Attention and Pattern Recognition

Attention and Pattern Recognition introduces the main psychological research on attention and the methods that have been used to study it. It also examines the subdivisions of focused and divided attention and explores how people recognise patterns and faces. The book is suitable for the AQA-A A2 level examination and students studying attention and pattern recognition for the first time at undergraduate level.

Nick Lund is a Senior Lecturer in Psychology at The Manchester Metropolitan University.

Routledge Modular Psychology

Series editors: Cara Flanagan is a Reviser for AS and A2 level Psychology and lectures at Inverness College. Philip Banyard is Associate Senior Lecturer in Psychology at Nottingham Trent University and a Chief Examiner for AS and A2 level Psychology. Both are experienced writers.

The *Routledge Modular Psychology* series is a completely new approach to introductory-level psychology, tailor-made to the new modular style of teaching. Each short book covers a topic in more detail than any large textbook can, allowing teacher and student to select material exactly to suit any particular course or project.

The books have been written especially for those students new to higher-level study, whether at school, college or university. They include specially designed features to help with technique, such as a model essay at an average level with an examiner's comments to show how extra marks can be gained. The authors are all examiners and teachers at the introductory level.

The *Routledge Modular Psychology* texts are all user-friendly and accessible and include the following features:

- practice essays with specialist commentary to show how to achieve a higher grade
- chapter summaries to assist with revision
- progress and review exercises
- glossary of key terms
- summaries of key research
- further reading to stimulate ongoing study and research
- cross-referencing to other books in the series

To my parents
John and Cyn Lund

Attention and
Pattern Recognition

Nick Lund

ROUTLEDGE
Taylor & Francis Group

First published 2001
by Routledge
27 Church Road, Hove, East Sussex BN3 2FA

Simultaneously published in the USA and Canada
by Taylor & Francis Inc.
325 Chestnut Street, Suite 800, Philadelphia, PA 19106

Routledge is an imprint of the Taylor & Francis Group

© 2001 Nick Lund

Typeset in Times and Frutiger by Keystroke,
Jacaranda Lodge, Wolverhampton
Printed and bound in Great Britain by
TJ International Ltd, Padstow, Cornwall

Cover design by Terry Foley

British Library Cataloguing in Publication Data
A catalogue record for this book is available from the British Library

Library of Congress Cataloging-in-Publication Data
Lund, Nick, 1956–
Attention and pattern recognition / Nick Lund.
p. cm. — (Routledge modular psychology)
Includes bibliographical references and index.
ISBN 0–415–23308–9 (hbk) —ISBN 0–415–23309–7 (pbk)
1. Attention. 2. Pattern perception. 3. Face perception.
I. Title. II. Series.
BF321 .L85 2001
152.14′23—dc21   00–051772

ISBN 0–415–23308–9 (hbk)
ISBN 0–415–23309–7 (pbk)

Contents

Figures

Acknowledgements

The series editors and Routledge acknowledge the expert help of Paul Humphreys, Examiner and Reviser for AS and A2 level Psychology, in compiling the Study aids chapter of each book in the series.

AQA (AEB) examination questions are reproduced by permission of the Assessment and Qualifications Alliance. The AQA do not accept responsibility for the answers or examiner comments in the Study aids chapter of this book or any other in the series.

Introduction

Attention and pattern recognition

The subject of this book, *Attention and Pattern Recognition*, comes under the Routledge Modular Psychology series that deals with **cognitive psychology**. Solso (1998) defines cognitive psychology as 'the scientific study of the thinking mind' and points out that it is concerned with a variety of areas of research including perception, pattern recognition, attention, memory, language and thinking. These research areas are closely related and there is considerable overlap between them. This is particularly true of attention, pattern recognition and perception. As Greene and Hicks (1984) point out: 'We can only perceive things we are attending to; we can only attend to things we perceive.'

Perception is concerned with how we interpret and experience information from our sense organs. Attention is largely the concentration on, and response to, part of the available information. Pattern recognition is the ability to pick out and organise some aspects of our visual input. Attention and pattern recognition are therefore closely linked since both involve selecting or focusing on part of our perceptual experiences. Treisman and Schmidt (1982) have argued that we should regard attention as 'perceptual glue' since it binds the features we perceive into coherent percepts of objects.

What is 'attention'?

William James (1890) wrote: 'Everyone knows what attention is. It is the taking possession by the mind, in clear and vivid form, of one out of what may seem several simultaneously possible objects or trains of thought. Focalisation, concentration of consciousness are of its essence.' While it is true that the term 'attention' is one that we all recognise and one that is in common usage (as in 'pay attention' or 'attention to detail'), psychologists find that it is a difficult concept to define. The James definition emphasises the focusing of attention or the concentration on one stimulus. This is echoed by a more recent definition by Solso (1998) who suggests that attention is 'the concentration of mental effort on sensory or mental events'.

However, part of the problem of definition is that the term 'attention' seems to refer to several different but interrelated abilities. It is probably a mistake to view attention as one ability. Allport (1993) believes that there is no uniform function to which we can attribute everything that has been labelled 'attention'. There seem to be at least two different areas of attention:

- **Focused (or selective) attention** – this is the ability to pick out (or focus on) some information from a mass of data. For example, in a crowded room there may be a hundred people talking yet you are able to listen to just one voice. This topic is the subject of Chapter 2.
- **Divided attention** – this is the ability to allocate attention to two or more tasks simultaneously. For example, an experienced driver may be able to attend to his/her driving, observe the obstacles and hazards around them and attend to a debate on the car radio. This topic is the subject of Chapter 3.

This distinction is useful when studying attention; however, in reality the difference between focused and divided attention is not clear-cut.

Somebody who is focusing their attention on writing an essay may find that they are also listening to a favourite song on the radio – their attention is now divided. Somebody who is dividing their attention between driving a car and having a conversation with a passenger will focus their attention entirely on their driving if a tyre bursts.

In addition to focused and divided attention there has been great interest in the role of practice in attention. This has led to ideas about whether tasks can be so well practised that they require no attentional resources. This has been labelled **automatic processing** and this is the subject of Chapter 4.

How is attention studied?

Although there have been numerous studies of attention, Eysenck (1984) suggests they can be divided into two basic experimental techniques:

1. **Dichotic listening task**. These are studies of auditory attention in which the participant is presented with two stimuli simultaneously. Typically one message is played to one ear and the second to the other ear through headphones. The participant is asked to select one of the messages (e.g. Cherry, 1953). As the nature of the task is to select (or to focus on) one stimulus, this technique has been used mainly to study **focused attention**. A common way of ensuring that the participants concentrated on and responded to one stimulus was to ask them to repeat one of the messages as it was played, a process which has been called **shadowing**. Although the participants were asked to focus on one stimulus, much of the interest of the researchers using this technique centred around what was noticed or understood about the rest of the stimuli.

2. **Dual task**. In these experiments participants are presented with two or more stimuli and are asked to attend or respond to all of them. As in the dichotic listening experiments, participants may be presented with two messages simultaneously, but in the dual task experiment they are asked to attend to both of them. The dual task experiments require the participant to try to attend to two or more stimuli simultaneously and are therefore frequently used in the study of **divided attention**. The ability to divide attention is affected by variables such as task difficulty and task similarity. Dual task

experiments therefore often use a variety of stimuli and tasks. For example, participants may be asked to shadow an auditory message and to search a visual scene.

These experimental techniques have been influential in the development of theories of attention. Other techniques have been used to study the application of attention research (or how attention affects everyday life). This includes the use of the **diary method** to record everyday mistakes caused by attention errors.

What are pattern and face recognition?

A vital aspect of both attention and perception is the ability to recognise and identify objects from the world around us. These objects range in complexity from a simple two-dimensional object on a page to the complex combination of features that constitute a face. Pattern recognition has been defined as 'the ability to abstract and integrate certain elements of a stimulus into an organised scheme for memory storage and retrieval' (Solso, 1998). Although the ability to recognise a letter on a page seems effortless and simple, it is a very difficult process to explain or understand. For example, the letter 'N' can be presented in hundreds of different ways, yet no matter what font is used in print everyone can recognise it as the same letter. Examiners see essays in hundreds of different types of handwriting but can decipher most of them. This poses the question of how these very different stimuli can be identified as the same object. Pattern recognition is the subject of Chapter 5.

Recognition and identification become more complex problems when we consider face recognition. When we think of a friend's face we tend to picture a stable image. However, in reality we do not receive a stable image to our eyes. For example, as your friend approaches you, the image of his/her face grows from a small dot when they are in the distance to an image which fills your field of view when they are close. As your friend moves around, sits down, stands up, etc., you will receive very different images of his/her face from different angles. Faces are mobile and vary in expression; a happy face is different from a sad face. Despite the huge variety of images we are presented with, the faces of friends seem to remain constant (see the topics of size and shape constancy in the book in this series on perception, by Rookes and Willson, 2000). Of course it does not have to be a friend's face; we can also recognise that several pictures of a stranger, which are taken from different angles, are of the same person. Face recognition is the subject of Chapter 6.

How are pattern and face recognition studied?

The complex processes involved in pattern and face recognition have been studied in a variety of ways:

1. **Behavioural studies**. In behavioural studies participants are typically presented with a pattern and the speed or accuracy of recognition is measured. The pattern to be detected is usually presented amongst a background of distracter stimuli. Face recognition is often studied by investigating how manipulation of an image of a face affects recognition. These types of experiment typically use human participants in a laboratory setting.
2. **Neurophysiological studies**. Another way of studying pattern recognition is to study the responses of the visual system to patterned visual stimuli. These studies usually look at the activities of the cells in the visual cortex. The firing rate of individual cells in response to different stimuli is recorded. Since this technique uses invasive surgery, this type of study uses non-human animals (primarily cats and monkeys) as participants. This type of technique is one method used in **cognitive neuroscience**. Cognitive neuroscience is the study of the structure and functioning of the brain to try to explain cognitive processes. In addition to recording the activity of single cells, cognitive neuroscientists study the general activity of the brain using techniques such as positron emission tomography (PET) and magnetic resonance imaging (MRI).
3. **Cognitive neuropsychology**. Cognitive neuropsychology is the study of the cognitive functioning of brain-injured patients. The aim is to investigate the patterns of impaired and normal performance to find the components of a model of normal functioning. For example, the condition **prosopagnosia** impairs the ability to recognise faces. However, prosopagnosia does not always affect people in the same way. Some people have problems in recognising familiar faces (including their own) but can recognise two different photographs of a stranger as the same person. Some people are

affected in completely the reverse fashion: they cannot match unfamiliar faces but can recognise familiar ones. These types of findings have very important implications for models of both pattern and face recognition.

One important distinction between pattern and face recognition is that the study of pattern recognition typically uses letters or numbers. These types of pattern are static and two-dimensional. Faces, on the other hand, are mobile and three-dimensional and we rarely see the same image of a face for long (people move, they talk, they show emotions, etc.). Therefore, although the study of face recognition does use drawings, any theory has to account for how this malleable and mobile 'pattern' is recognised.

The information processing approach

Information processing is one of the central concepts of all cognitive psychology. The information processing approach lies at the heart of the study of memory, language, thought, perception, pattern recognition and attention. This approach uses analogies from computer science to try to explain cognitive processes. It assumes that perception, memory, attention, etc. are not immediate results of stimulation but that they occur as a result of processing information over time. The cognitive psychologists' aims are to study and explain these processes. The processes involved in, for example, attention and memory may be different, but the information processing approach suggests that all cognitive abilities have three main stages:

- input – this is the reception or recording of information
- translation – this is the manipulation of information and may involve categorising data, storing data, interpreting data, etc.
- output – this is the response to the information

Each of these stages could involve a number of processes. Part of the translation process in attention, for example, might involve physical analysis followed by semantic analysis of data. Early cognitive models, which were based on the computer technology of the time, tend to be based on the idea of **serial processing**. This assumes that information has to be processed in sequence in a step-by-step fashion. If there are several sets of information to be processed – for example, when there are two messages – serial processing assumes that they will be dealt with one at a time. A good example of a serial processing theory is Broadbent's filter model of attention (see p. 12). As computer programs became more complex, and, more recently, with the development of neural networks, cognitive psychologists began to develop models based on **parallel processing**. This assumes that two or more inputs can be dealt with at the same time. Allport's module model of attention is a good example of the use of parallel processing (see p. 32).

One consequence of the information processing approach has been the development of computer models of cognitive abilities. This is particularly true of pattern and face recognition where computer models not only have scientific interest but also have important applications (e.g. the computer recognition of postcodes on letters).

Summary

Attention and pattern recognition are two cognitive processes which have close links with memory and perception. Attention is the concentration of mental effort on either external stimuli or thoughts. One aspect of attention is focused attention. This is the ability to select some information from a mass of stimuli, and it has been studied using dichotic listening task experiments. Divided attention is the ability to attend to two or more tasks at the same time and has largely been studied using dual task experiments. Studies of the effect of practice on attention have led to theories of automatic processing. This is the idea that some tasks become so well practised that they require no attention. The study of pattern recognition looks at the ability to pick out certain stimuli and match them with information stored in memory. Although faces might be regarded as complex patterns, the study of face recognition has become a separate field of study, partly because faces are very significant in our social interactions. Pattern and face recognition have been studied using behavioural studies, neurophysiological studies and cognitive neuropsychology. The theories of attention and pattern recognition have been greatly influenced by the information processing approach which uses analogies from computer science to explain cognitive processes.

Review exercise

Briefly differentiate between the following pairs of terms:

Focused attention and divided attention
Dichotic listening task and dual task
Neurophysiological studies and cognitive neuropsychology
Serial processing and parallel processing

Further reading

Solso, R.L. (1998) *Cognitive Psychology* (5th edn). Boston: Allyn and Bacon. This is a good cognitive psychology textbook which has a chapter on pattern recognition and another on attention. Although primarily aimed at undergraduate level it is very easy to read.

2

Focused attention

Introduction

We are constantly bombarded with stimuli of all sorts: an ever-changing visual scene, numerous sounds, tastes, smells and even the touch of our clothes. Yet although there is a mass of stimuli around us we are usually only aware of a small fraction of it. Try sitting quietly and try to take note of all the sounds that you can hear. Did you notice any that you were not aware of a few minutes ago? We are able to select some information whilst apparently ignoring the rest. For example, we can listen to one person in a crowded room but ignore the hubbub of conversation around us. This ability is referred to as focused (or selective) attention.

Focused attention – early research

All of the theories in this chapter can trace their origins to Broadbent's very influential book *Perception and Communication* (1958). This book stimulated the modern studies of attention and had a deep impact on cognitive psychology as a whole. Broadbent brought a new way of looking at cognitive abilities and his ideas were influenced by a number of key experiments such as those by Cherry (1953) and his own (Broadbent, 1954).

Cocktail party phenomenon

Cherry began by investigating the 'cocktail party phenomenon'. This can occur at any busy social gathering such as a cocktail party. It had been noticed that in a busy room full of different conversations people have the ability to pick out one conversation and concentrate on it (or attend to it) whilst ignoring the rest. However, if someone else in the room started to talk about that person or to mention their name several times they often noticed and switched their attention to the other conversation. Cherry tried to investigate this phenomenon experimentally. In some experiments he asked participants to try to analyse one of several messages being played to both ears over headphones. His most fruitful research, however, came from using **dichotic listening tasks**. In these experiments participants were played two different messages simultaneously. One message was played to the right ear and the other to the left ear. Cherry asked participants to repeat one of the messages out loud, a procedure known as **shadowing**. This proved to be a fairly easy task and participants were able to understand the shadowed message and could answer questions about it (in essence this is what we do every day as we sift one message from the variety of sounds around us). However, participants had no idea what the other message was about and could not answer questions about it. They were aware of the *physical qualities* of the message such as whether it was spoken by a man or a woman, or whether it was a voice or a tone, but the meaning of the message (the *semantic content*) was lost. This suggests that the messages were processed in a number of stages and that, in the early stage, when the physical properties of the message are being processed, several messages can be analysed. However, in the later stages, when the meaning of the message is being processed, only one message can be analysed at once.

'Channels' of attention

Broadbent (1954) also used headphones to play messages to each ear, but his studies used the **split-span procedure** (Figure 2.1). In these experiments participants heard a series of three numbers in each ear. Different numbers were played simultaneously to either ear. In Figure 2.1 the number 5 is played in the left ear as the number 2 is played in the right.

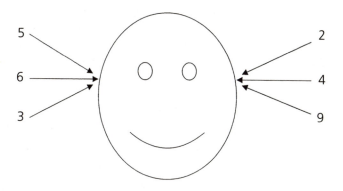

Figure 2.1 **The split-span procedure**

Participants were then asked to recall the numbers in one of two ways, pair-by-pair (i.e. 5–2, 6–4 and 3–9) or ear-by-ear (i.e. 5–6–3 and 2–4–9). The ear-by-ear condition was found to be both easier and more accurate to recall (with 65 per cent recall as compared to 20 per cent for the pair-by-pair condition). Broadbent thought that this suggested that the ears act as two different 'channels' and that it takes time to switch from one channel to the other. Analysing first one ear (or channel) then the other is easier than switching from ear to ear (channel to channel) several times as is necessary in the pair-by-pair condition.

These early findings led to a number of models of focused attention. These are all described as **single channel models** because they all proposed that, at some point, information is filtered in some way. The differences between the models centre on the *location* and *function* of the filter.

Broadbent's theory – the filter model

In *Perception and Communication* (1958) Broadbent tried to explain the results of both his own and Cherry's experiments. His 'filter model' of attention was the first modern theory of attention and introduced a number of key concepts. One of the ideas was that people are limited in their ability to process information. Broadbent claimed that the experimental evidence suggested that attention has a **limited capacity**. (For example, in a crowded room we cannot listen to every conversation at once. As we can only listen to one conversation at a time our attention is limited in capacity.) The other key element of the theory is the **filter**. Since our attention is limited in capacity Broadbent proposed that there is a filter which allows some information through, but blocks out the rest. The detail of the filter model is shown in Figure 2.2.

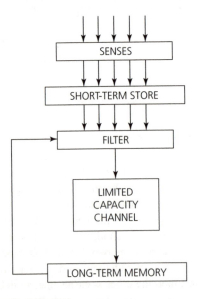

Figure 2.2 **The filter model**

In the diagram the arrows represent flow of information and each box shows a stage of processing. The first stage of processing the information for attention is the senses (eyes, ears, etc.), which gather data from the world around us. In the diagram the first five arrows could represent five conversations that can be detected. The senses process the information and pass it to a short-term store. This acts as a 'buffer' in the system and keeps the information for a brief time until it is either processed or decays (fades from the store). The information then proceeds to the filter. This is a vital stage because it is the filter that allows some stimuli through for semantic processing and blocks out the rest. The filter is selective and can pick out information based on the physical characteristics of the stimuli. These physical characteristics could be the sound of a friend's voice. Thus in Figure 2.2 the sounds of five voices reach the filter but only one is selected for further attention. The filter is necessary because the information then passes to a **limited capacity channel**. This is essentially a bottleneck that can only allow a limited flow of information for semantic analysis – the information that we pay attention to. Broadbent's theory also recognises that we can change the bias in our filter to allow different information through. This means the filter can be 're-tuned' to allow another voice through it, so that in a crowded room we can attend to first one conversation then another.

This model of attention is described as an **early selection model** because the filter selects information at an early stage of processing the information.

Evaluation of the filter model

Broadbent's theory appears to explain some of the early research findings well. For example, the results of Cherry's dichotic listening tasks suggest that we can only attend to one voice at a time. In his studies the semantic content of the information going to the unattended ear was lost (only some physical characteristics were noticed). This is exactly what the filter model would predict since the filter should block the information from the unattended ear.

However, soon after its publication it became clear that Broadbent's theory was flawed. The theory does not adequately explain the 'cocktail party phenomenon' (see p. 10). It does explain how we could listen to one person at a party while we block out all other conversations. However, it does not explain how we notice when someone else mentions our name or something of interest. Clearly if we notice, or switch attention to, another conversation it was *not* blocked by the filter. The theory also has difficulty in explaining a variety of experimental findings. Moray (1959) used the dichotic listening procedure to present participants with two messages. The participants were asked to shadow one message. Moray adapted the other message (the 'unattended' message) so that it contained several references to the participant's name. Although they did not notice every reference to them, the participants noticed their name about a third of the time. The filter was obviously not blocking the unattended message.

Gray and Wedderburn (1960) studied attention by using a variation of the split-span procedure. Instead of using numbers (as Broadbent had done) Gray and Wedderburn presented either different short phrases to each ear simultaneously or different syllables to each ear simultaneously. For example, in one experiment, participants were presented with:

OB-2-TIVE   in the left ear
6-JEC-9   in the right ear

Participants were asked to shadow the left ear and, if Broadbent's theory is correct, they should have heard 'ob-two-tive' since the right ear (the unattended channel) should have been blocked out. However, most reported hearing 'ob-jec-tive' even though the syllable 'jec' was played to the right ear. Gray and Wedderburn also used short phrases instead of fragments of words. For example, in one ear participants were presented with 'Dear-4-Jane' and in the other '8-Aunt-2'. Participants often reported hearing 'Dear Aunt Jane'. These experiments seem to suggest that attention is more complicated than a simple filtering process. Another aspect of the attention process seems to be to actively search the environment to make sense of the information. Treisman (1964) found that if bilingual participants shadowed a message in English in one ear and the same message was played in French in the other ear they would frequently notice that the messages were the same. This indicates that the unattended ear was being monitored to some extent.

Later research also questioned the validity of some of the assumptions about the early experiments. For example, most of the early studies that used shadowing suggested that the participants noticed little information in the non-shadowed ear. Broadbent assumed that this was because the information was not processed (it had been filtered). However, an alternative explanation is that the task was unfamiliar and therefore difficult (see controlled vs. automatic processing, p. 44).

Underwood (1974) found that, while it was true that inexperienced participants were poor at detecting digits in an unattended ear, experienced participants were capable of a much better performance (with an 8 per cent and 67 per cent success rate respectively). The early studies may not have shown a limit to the participants' attention but rather a lack of practice of an unfamiliar task.

Review Broadbent's theory by answering the following questions:

1. Why is the filter necessary?
2. What does the filter do?
3. Why is the theory described as an early filter model?
4. Name one experiment that supports Broadbent's theory.
5. Describe one experiment that Broadbent's theory cannot explain.

Progress exercise

Treisman's theory – the attenuator model

Treisman's attenuator model is largely an adaptation of Broadbent's theory. Although she recognised the problems of the Broadbent model, Treisman (1964) accepted many of the key assumptions that he made and used a lot of the same structures (the same architecture) in her model. The major modification in the attenuator model is in the function of the filter. Treisman suggested that the filter does not block rejected information but the information is attenuated (or turned down). Hence some information is selected for semantic analysis and passes through the filter at full strength, and the remaining stimuli are passed through the filter in a weakened form (see Figure 2.3).

After the attenuator the information goes through 'semantic analysis', that is, the information is analysed according to word meaning, grammatical structure and sentence meaning. Normally this analysis will be of the selected information (or the stimuli passing through the filter at 'full volume'). Occasionally some of the rejected, or attenuated, information will be analysed if this information is important or highly relevant. However, this raises an important question. If the information is attenuated, how do we know that it is important or relevant? Treisman suggested that we have 'word units' which we use when analysing and recognising sentences. These word

15

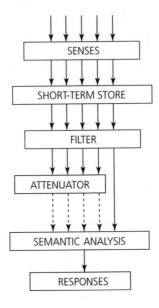

Figure 2.3 **The attenuator model**

units vary in thresholds. This means that they require different intensity of stimuli to activate them. Some words, such as our names, have very low thresholds – they are easily activated. Other words have high thresholds because they are not relevant to us or are not interesting – they are not easily activated. This means that sometimes even if information is attenuated it may activate a word unit. In the example of the cocktail party we notice a different conversation when someone mentions our name. This is because our names are very important to us and even though it is attenuated it is enough to activate the word unit. Treisman also suggested that the thresholds of word units vary with expectation and context. When a word is expected it momentarily has a lower threshold and will be easily activated.

The attenuator model is another **early selection model** since the filter selects information at an early stage of analysis.

Evaluation of the attenuator model

The attenuator model is more flexible than the filter model and is better able to explain the experimental evidence discussed so far. For example, Moray (1959) found that participants noticed their names in a non-shadowed ear about a third of the time. The attenuator model would suggest that this is because the information in the non-shadowed ear is attenuated and therefore not usually noticed. However, since the participant's name has such a low threshold it is sometimes detected. The Gray and Wedderburn (1960) study suggested that participants could switch their attention to make sense of information. So when 'Dear-4-Jane' was played in one ear and '8-Aunt-2' was played in the other, participants heard 'Dear Aunt Jane'. Treisman would argue that this is because, at the moment '4' and 'Aunt' are played, participants expect to hear a word like Aunt and it momentarily has a low threshold.

However, there are a number of theoretical problems with the attenuator model. First, the model suggests that selection is early and that some information is then processed semantically and some is attenuated. However one of Treisman's experiments suggests that there is more semantic analysis of the attenuated information than the model allows. She found that if bilingual participants shadowed a message in English in one ear they would often notice if the same message was played in French in the other ear. If participants are able to recognise that two messages are identical in content but are in different languages, then presumably both are being analysed semantically. Secondly, there is a question of how a filter which is so early in the system can make the decisions about what should and should not be attenuated.

Write brief notes on the following:

1. What is the function of an attenuator?
2. Why do some words attract our attention more than others do?
3. Why does the attenuator model explain the cocktail party phenomenon better than the filter model?

Progress exercise

Deutsch and Deutsch – the pertinence model

The pertinence model was first proposed by Deutsch and Deutsch in 1963 and was revised several times by Norman (1969, 1976). This model introduces the idea of **late selection** and puts the bottleneck of processing information later than the attenuator model does. The pertinence model suggests that *all* information is initially processed and that selection only takes place after each input (or message) has been analysed in the memory system. In this model, selection for attention is closer to the responses (output) than the senses (input). Selection then takes place based on the pertinence of the information. Information that is the most pertinent (e.g. relevant and/or important) is most likely to be selected (see Figure 2.4).

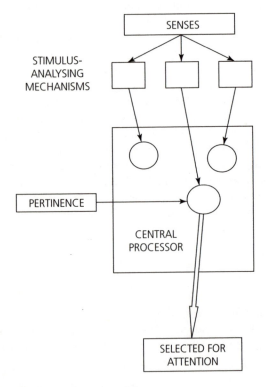

Figure 2.4 **The pertinence model**

The pertinence of information is influenced by factors such as expectations and context (these are called top-down factors, see p. 63).

Evaluation of the pertinence model

There is some support for the pertinence model from research that shows that information in an 'unattended' message is processed and analysed. MacKay (1973) found that, when participants were asked to shadow an ambiguous sentence in one ear, the perception of the meaning of the sentence was influenced by the message in the other ear. For instance, participants shadowed the sentence 'They were throwing stones at the bank', and at the same time the word 'river' or 'money' was played in the other ear. If the word 'river' was played, participants believed that 'bank' referred to a riverbank, but if the word 'money' was played they believed that it referred to a high street bank. Although participants reported that they were not consciously aware of the word in the unattended ear it must have been analysed since it influenced the interpretation of the shadowed message.

A *potentially* serious problem of this model is the finding that the information from most unattended messages is completely lost (e.g. Cherry, 1953). If it is all analysed then why do participants find it impossible to recall any semantic content? Norman (1969) has suggested that this is because the information is stored in short-term memory and is forgotten very quickly. He found that participants *could* remember the last few words of an unattended message if asked to recall them immediately after the message ended. (In most experiments the participants are asked to recall the information after they have finished shadowing and, since this carries on after the messages have finished, the unattended message has been forgotten.)

However, there are a number of other problems with the pertinence model. As Solso (1979) points out, this model is uneconomical. It suggests that *all* information is analysed for meaning, yet most of it would not be required or used. In addition, if all incoming information is analysed then we would need a very large processing capacity.

Most of the experimental evidence discussed so far indicates that information in the unattended ear is processed to some degree. Both the Treisman and the Deutsch and Deutsch models can explain this. The essential difference between the models is where the selection for further attention takes place – early (in the Treisman model) or late (in the Deutsch and Deutsch model). Research by Treisman and Geffen (1967) was designed to test where selection took place. They asked participants to shadow a message in one ear and at the same time to try to detect a target word that could occur in the messages to either ear. If, for example, the target word was 'cat', participants were instructed to try to detect the word 'cat' in both the shadowed and non-shadowed message. Treisman and Geffen argued that the Treisman model predicts that the target word would be detected more in the shadowed ear than in the unattended ear (since information in the shadowed message is not attenuated but all other information is attenuated). They suggested that the Deutsch and Deutsch model predicts that the target word would be detected equally in both ears (since the target word is equally pertinent in any message). They found that the target word was detected 87 per cent of the time in the shadowed ear but only 8 per cent in the unattended ear. This seems to be evidence of an early selection process.

However, Deutsch and Deutsch (1967) have claimed that this conclusion is based on a false premise. Treisman and Geffen assumed that the Deutsch and Deutsch model predicts that the target word was equally pertinent in both the shadowed and non-shadowed message. Deutsch and Deutsch claim that this is not true. Participants are asked to detect a target word in the non-shadowed ear but they are asked to detect a target word *and* shadow the whole message in the shadowed ear. Hence any information in this ear becomes more pertinent.

Early or late selection?

All of the theories of focused attention assume that there is a single filtering process involved at some stage of attention. However, evidence seems to indicate that focused attention involves both early and late selection of information. Johnson and Heinz (1978) have proposed an alternative theory that suggests there are a number of *different stages* of processing for incoming information. Each of these stages uses some of the available processing capacity. Therefore, to avoid overloading our limited capacity, unattended stimuli are processed at the minimum level required to perform a task. In order to test this theory Johnson and Heinz (1979) asked participants to shadow one set of words while ignoring another set. In one condition one set of words was spoken by a man and the other by a woman (this was the easy condition). In the difficult condition the same man spoke both sets of words. In the easy condition it was a simple process to separate the two sets of words since the physical characteristics of the voices differed. When participants were asked to shadow the male voice they did not have to process the words spoken by the female voice. However, in the difficult condition participants could not differentiate the two sets of words by the physical characteristics alone. The unattended message needed to be processed to a greater degree. As predicted by their theory, Johnson and Heinz found that, when given an unexpected memory test of the unattended words, participants recalled more in the difficult condition. This seems to indicate that selection can be *early* if information can be processed using physical properties (i.e. the easy condition), or selection might be *late* if the information needs more thorough analysis (i.e. the difficult condition).

Evaluation of single channel models

There is now considerable doubt whether any simple single channel model can explain the complex processes involved in attention (e.g. Allport, 1980). The models of focused attention assume that there is a single processor that deals with all incoming information and this is why, for example, we cannot listen to two messages at once. However, dual task experiments show that we are capable of doing several complex tasks at once (e.g. driving and talking). The models of focused attention ignore vital factors such as levels of arousal, task difficulty, practice, etc. These factors are better explained by theories that try to explain how we are able to do several tasks at once (or theories of **divided attention**, which are discussed in the next chapter).

Another obvious criticism of the focused attention theories discussed in this chapter is that they all concentrate on research from auditory attention. This of course ignores other forms of attention such as visual attention. It is probable that the process of attention is different for different senses/abilities. For example, an assumption of the focused attention theories is that the left and right ears can act as separate channels for incoming information. This is not true for vision, since eyes seem to act as one channel. We cannot look at one scene with our left eye and another with our right. We focus both our eyes on one scene. The studies of visual attention have led to an entirely different type of explanation of focused attention, such as Eriksen's zoom-lens theory and Treisman's feature integration theory. It may be better to regard attention as a number of different processes (e.g. auditory, visual, etc.) rather than one (Allport, 1993).

Summary

After early research into the cocktail party phenomenon a number of theories of focused attention were proposed. Broadbent proposed an early filter model. This suggests that there is a selective filter that blocks out some information but allows the required information through to a limited capacity channel. However, this does not explain the cocktail party phenomenon. Treisman believed that the filter was more flexible and that rejected information was not blocked but was attenuated. Since rejected information was available for semantic analysis (in a weakened form) important information could be detected. Although this theory does explain the cocktail party phenomenon it does not explain how this early filter is able to make decisions about which information should be attenuated. Deutsch and Deutsch proposed a late selection model in which all information is initially processed and then selection takes place based on the pertinence of information. This explains much of the research evidence but it is an uneconomical model (why analyse all information if only a small proportion is to be used?). These simple single channel models do not seem to explain the complexities of focused attention.

Look at the research/concept on the left and, with the aid of the chapter, summarise it in a few key words.

Review exercise	
Cocktail party phenomenon	
Limited capacity channel	
Dichotic listening task	
Early selection	
Late selection	
Attenuate	
Single channel theory	
Shadowing	
Pertinence	

Further reading

Eysenck, M.W. and Keane, M.T. (1995) *Cognitive Psychology – A Student's Handbook* (3rd edn). Hove, UK: Lawrence Erlbaum Associates Ltd. This is a standard cognitive psychology textbook for many undergraduate courses. Chapter 5 provides a very clear discussion of most aspects of attention, including focused attention.

Hampson, P.J. and Morris, P.E. (1996) *Understanding Cognition*. Oxford: Blackwell. Chapter 5 has a good discussion of attention and has a section on focused attention.

3

Divided attention

Introduction

Although most of the research of focused attention implies that participants have difficulty in doing two things at once, our everyday experience suggests otherwise. We frequently have to do several things at the same time and we often think about a number of things at once. Students can listen to a lecturer and at the same time make notes on what the lecturer has said a few moments earlier. When making a meal most people can think about the progress of a number of dishes (e.g. the vegetables) and yet can still be preparing another (e.g. a sauce). There are a number of studies which show that people have the ability to do several complex tasks simultaneously. For example, in one study pianists shadowed speech whilst simultaneously sight-reading music

(Allport *et al.*, 1972). The ability to do several tasks at once is referred to as divided attention and is usually studied using dual task experiments.

Dual task experiments

One problem with the study of focused attention is that the research concentrated on a limited research technique, the dichotic listening technique. This caused a number of crucial factors to be ignored or overlooked. Eysenck and Keane (1995) have identified three major factors that affect the ability to do two or more tasks at once:

1. **Task similarity**

   There is a lot of evidence which indicates that the ability to do two tasks at once is affected greatly by the similarity of the two tasks. It is difficult to do two very similar tasks at the same time. Participants find it much easier to do two dissimilar tasks at once. A very good example of this was shown by Allport *et al.* (1972), which is described in Key research summary 1 on p. 105. Three groups of participants were asked to shadow prose that was played in one ear using headphones and at the same time to learn a list. The first group tried to learn a list of words that was presented to the other ear. The second group tried to learn the same list but in this condition the words were printed on a screen. The third group tried to learn the same list, this time presented as pictures on a screen. Recall of the list in condition one, where the participants were trying to listen to prose and listen to the list of words, was very poor. However, recall in condition three, where participants were listening to prose and looking at pictures, was very good. Although similarity seems to be an important factor in dual task experiments it is a difficult concept to define and consequently it is difficult to measure. For example, reading a novel and listening to a novel that has been recorded on tape may seem similar but may require different processes. Conversely, playing a video game and flying a jet aircraft do not initially seem similar but can require the same type of skills.

2. **Task difficulty**

   It seems self-evident that it is easier to do two simple tasks at once than two complex tasks at once. This is an important factor in dual task experiments, but difficulty, like similarity, is a hard concept to quantify. A difficult task for one person may be a relatively easy one for another. An experienced typist may be able to copy this paragraph with ease whilst having a conversation. An inexperienced typist would find copying difficult and would have to concentrate on the keyboard. Difficulty of a task may change for an individual over time. Skills such as typing and driving become easier with practice. Practice seems to reduce the difficulty of some tasks (see below). Another problem with the concept of difficulty is that something that seems simple when done by itself may become difficult when trying to combine it with a second task.

3. **Practice**

Practice improves performance in many dual task experiments. Tasks that seem impossible at first, such as attending to two different messages, become possible with practice. A good demonstration of this was shown by Spelke *et al*. (1976). They asked two students to write down dictated words while reading short stories. Initially they found that it was very difficult to combine these two tasks and their handwriting, reading speed and comprehension were all impaired. However, after only thirty hours' training, their reading speed and comprehension were unaffected by the dictation task. There may be a number of reasons why practice improves performance in dual task experiments. One is that practice may reduce the amount of resources a task uses (see automatic processing, p. 42). Another reason is that practice may help participants learn strategies to deal with the competing demands of two tasks.

Despite the problems of quantifying these factors, they are important considerations for any theory of divided attention. The limited capacity theories (e.g. Kahneman, Norman and Bobrow) have concentrated on the influence of task difficulty and practice, whereas the multiple channel theories (e.g. Allport, Navon and Gopher) stress the role of task similarity in divided attention.

Kahneman – central capacity theory

Kahneman (1973) has proposed a limited capacity model of attention which has a **central processor** that allocates attention (see Figure 3.1).

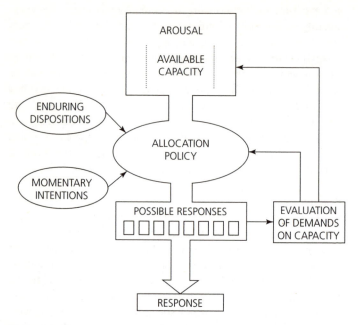

Figure 3.1 **The central capacity model of divided attention**

He views attention as a skill rather than a process. This theory claims that people are sometimes capable of performing two or more tasks at a time depending on the available capacity and the nature of the tasks. Kahneman introduced the idea of parallel processing in attention (in contrast to the models of focused attention, which concentrated on serial processing). The model suggests that capacity is not fixed but varies with arousal. We have more capacity available when we are awake and fully alert than when we are tired or 'half asleep'. Tasks require different processing capacity and Kahneman referred to this as **mental effort**. The amount of mental effort required by a task depends upon the **difficulty** of the task and the degree of **practice** that an individual has of it. Some tasks are easy and, since they require little effort, they leave a lot of spare capacity. Other tasks are difficult and leave very little spare capacity because they require great mental effort. For example, it is easy to think of other things (daydream) while cycling, but when concentrating on writing an essay in an exam it is difficult to think of anything except the essay. This theory predicts that tasks require less mental effort with practice and consequently they will take up less of the available capacity.

A central feature of the capacity model is the need to allocate the available capacity. The **allocation of attention** is determined by a combination of various factors such as 'momentary intentions' and 'enduring dispositions'. **Momentary intentions** are factors that are important at any particular time. For example, if you are in a conversation you want to pay attention to one person, or if you are driving you need to pay attention to the road. **Enduring dispositions** are factors that are always important. These may be biological (if you accidentally place your hand on a hot object it will 'grab' your attention) or learned (if somebody shouts your name it will grab your attention). These two factors interact and often the enduring dispositions will override the momentary intentions. For example, you may be listening to one person (a momentary intention) but if someone else shouts your name your attention shifts (because of an enduring disposition).

Another very important element in the allocation of attention is an **evaluation of demands on capacity**. When tasks leave spare capacity the allocation policy can remain unchanged, but if demands of several tasks are too high then the allocation has to be changed. In other words we have to decide on which task(s) to attend to. This theory suggests that it is possible to divide attention between tasks provided the capacity of the central processor is not exceeded. It is possible to do two simple tasks because they do not overload the capacity, but we may not have the capacity for two difficult tasks. It is possible to walk with a friend and talk to them simultaneously because neither task requires much mental effort. It is not possible to shadow a message and write an essay simultaneously because they both require a lot of our attention resources. Tasks such as essay writing require all the available mental effort and therefore require undivided (or focused) attention. Kahneman's model seeks to explain both divided and focused attention and illustrates the somewhat artificial distinction between the two.

Evaluation of central capacity theory

Kahneman's model of a central processor that allocates attention resources is more flexible than focused attention models. It can explain the findings of both the dichotic listening experiments and the dual task experiments (i.e. focused and divided attention). This model also attempts to incorporate a number of crucial variables which the focused attention models ignored, such as task difficulty, the role of practice and arousal. It accounts for findings which show that novices have difficulty in performing dual task experiments but experienced participants do not (e.g. Spelke *et al.*, 1976) since it predicts that practice reduces the demands of a task.

However, despite its flexibility there are a number of problems with this model. First, it is not very specific about the limits of capacity. Although there do seem to be limits to our attention capacity it is difficult to define these limits. Studies such as that of Spelke *et al.* (1976) imply that the limit may be larger than most researchers assumed. Another criticism of the model is that it offers a superficial explanation of the processes involved (Allport, 1980). Allport claims that the model 'merely soothes away curiosity by the appearance of providing an explanation'.

The most serious problem of the model is that it does not adequately explain the strong influence of similarity in dual task studies. The Kahneman model proposes that we have a limited capacity which is allocated by a single central processor. This implies that any two tasks will interfere with each other if the capacity needed for them exceeds the available capacity. However, a number of studies suggest it is not the *difficulty* (and therefore capacity) but the degree of *similarity* of the two tasks that is the most important factor in dual task performance (e.g. Wickens *et al.*, 1983). These findings have led Payne and Wenger (1998) to conclude that 'one or more of the assumptions underlying the single capacity model of Kahneman are invalid'. The results of the influence of similarity are better explained by multiple channel theories (see p. 32) which take the view that 'attention' should be seen as a number of separate resources each with its own capacity.

Norman and Bobrow – central capacity interference theory

Like Kahneman, Norman and Bobrow (1975) have proposed that attention is limited in capacity and is controlled centrally. However, Norman and Bobrow claim that performance of attention tasks can only be explained by two types of limitation on performance. Their theory introduces a distinction between **resource-limited** and **data-limited** processes. Some tasks can be improved by allocating more resources to them. However, for complex tasks there is a point where no more resources are available and performance cannot be improved. These tasks are resource-limited. Other tasks cannot be improved with more resources because it is the data that are limited. For example, if you cannot hear someone on a poor telephone connection you will not improve performance by allocating more and more resources. The only way to improve performance would be to get a better connection. In this situation attention is data-limited.

Evaluation of central capacity interference theory

The idea that attention performance may be limited in two ways, either by central resources or by the quality of the data, seems to explain many of the research findings from both dichotic listening task and dual task experiments. For example, Cherry (1953) found that when participants were shadowing a message in one ear they noticed very little about the content of the other ear (often to the extent that they did not recognise that it was reverse speech or a foreign language). However, they did notice when a pure tone was inserted into the non-shadowed message. This could be because tones do not need many resources to detect them (they are data-limited). Spoken messages require processing resources and, since the shadowed message requires these resources, there is no spare capacity to analyse speech in the non-shadowed ear (because it is resource-limited).

The problem with this theory is its failure to predict performance of tasks in experiments. It can 'explain' the results of experiments once the findings are known. Hampson and Morris (1996) claim:

it is only after knowing how a particular experiment turned out that we can claim that one process is data limited and the other is resource limited. We distinguish between the processes on the basis of the results and then 'explain' the results using our distinction between two sorts of process, and a classic circular argument results.

The theory is difficult to test because of its failure to predict findings and has been described as non-falsifiable. No experiment could provide evidence against the theory.

Progress exercise

Identify whether the following tasks would be resource-limited or data-limited:

1. Trying to identify a friend on a poor-quality video recording.
2. Trying to listen to two separate conversations.
3. Learning to ride a unicycle and juggle at the same time.
4. Trying to listen to your teacher when all the people near you are talking.

Multiple channel theories

Some cognitive psychologists doubt whether a limited capacity model with a central processor can explain the complex nature of attention (Neisser, 1976; Allport, 1993). There is doubt whether a single limited capacity processor could deal with the many different types of task required by an attentional system. There is also doubt whether the brain could have a single filter to deal with all attentional tasks. As Hampson and Morris (1996) have pointed out, 'it is difficult to see how the neurology of the brain could produce a system of processing capacity that was completely open to use in any of the tasks that might be presented'.

Another major problem is that these models do not adequately explain why task similarity is such a major factor in dual task experiments. For example, Allport *et al.* (1972) found that participants could not learn a list presented verbally via one ear on headphones while they were shadowing a message in the other ear. However, they could learn the list when it was presented as pictures on a screen and simultaneously shadow a message. Presumably learning a list presented orally or pictorially uses a similar amount of resources, so why is one condition so much more difficult than the other? One explanation is that trying to listen to two competing messages taxes our auditory attention but listening to a message does not stop us noticing visual input. These findings are better explained by theories that propose separate resources for different aspects of attention.

Allport – modules of attention

Allport (1980, 1993) has proposed that attention consists of a number of specialised **modules**. Each module deals with a different ability or skill, so that one module may deal with auditory information, another with visual information, etc. Allport suggests that each module has its own resources and each has a limited capacity. (This is in contrast to capacity theories that regard attention as being controlled by one central processor with a single limited capacity.) Allport's theory predicts that similarity will be a major factor in the performance of dual task experiments (see Figure 3.2). When tasks are similar they compete for the resources of one module and interfere with each other. This makes it difficult to perform them simultaneously. However, dissimilar tasks use different modules and do not require the same resources. These tasks do not interfere with each other and may be performed simultaneously (they are processed in parallel).

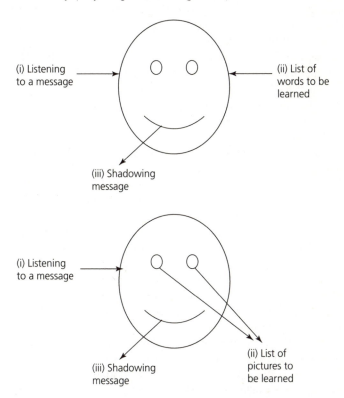

Figure 3.2 **The effect of similarity on the ability to perform a number of tasks**

Wickens (1984) supports the idea of modules and after reviewing the evidence has suggested that different modules may deal with different aspects of a task. He proposes that modules (or attentional resources) exist for input mode (e.g. vision, hearing), processing mechanism (e.g. speech recognition, decision making) and output mode (e.g. speaking, manual).

Evaluation of module theory

The notion that attentional processes use a number of different modules seems to explain the effects of similarity in dual task experiments. Allport *et al.* (1972) found that when participants were shadowing a message presented via headphones they could not learn a list presented in the other ear. This is because the auditory module was overloaded. However, if the list was presented as pictures, participants learned the list well. In this condition listening to the message on headphones uses the auditory module and learning pictures uses the visual module. Treisman and Davies (1973) have reported similar results. They found that when two tasks require monitoring of the inputs from the same sense modalities, then performance is far worse than when two different modalities are used.

The concept of modules has also received support from cognitive neuropsychology. One of the fundamental assumptions of cognitive neuropsychology is that there are 'relatively independent cognitive processors or modules, each of which can function to some extent in isolation from the rest of the processing system; brain damage will typically impair only some of these modules' (Eysenck and Keane, 1995). This approach has identified a number of syndromes that impair the functioning of some aspects but not others. For example, there are a number of types of aphasia (disorders of language), some of which affect the understanding of spoken words, others written words and some the production of spoken words. This is consistent with the idea of different processing modules.

One of the main problems of the theory is that it does not specify the number of modules or precisely what types of modules they are. This makes it difficult to test the model since virtually any finding from dual task experiments can be explained by proposing the existence of another module. When it is found that two tasks interfere with each other this can be explained by claiming they use the same module at some point. If the two tasks do not interfere with each other it can now be claimed that they use different modules. The theory is therefore non-falsifiable.

Another major problem is the question of how the modules work together. Somebody who is holding a conversation while driving may be using a variety of modules: one dealing with visual input, one dealing with auditory input, one dealing with speech and another dealing with manual skills. The person deals with these different skills in a highly integrated fashion, but the theory does not explain how the modules are co-ordinated. Finally, some studies have shown that similar tasks can be performed simultaneously if participants are given enough practice (e.g. Underwood, 1974; Spelke *et al.*, 1976). Presumably, even with practice, similar tasks are still competing for the resources of one module.

Navon and Gopher – multiple resource theory

Navon and Gopher (1979) have proposed a **multiple resource** model of attention. This approach suggests that attentional processes use a number of specialised 'mental resources'. In essence these are very similar to the concept of modules. One difference from the modular approach is that the multiple resource model claims that in some cases performance on one task can be traded for performance levels on another.

Navon and Gopher use economic concepts such as supply and demand to explain divided attention. They use the analogy of a manufacturer to describe the cognitive system. In any manufacturing process there is an input, the raw goods, a transformation in which the raw goods are changed in some way, and an output, the finished product. This corresponds with the stimuli (input), the processing of the information (transformation), and the response (output). When there are enough tools to deal with the raw goods, production can proceed. However, if there are not enough tools to deal with the raw goods then the manufacturing process will slow down. Similarly when we do not have enough cognitive resources to deal with the input our cognitive processes slow down.

Imagine a manufacturing process that requires a powerful drill. If all the goods need this drill the processing will be slowed down. There may be many other tools available, such as saws and lathes, but since most of them cannot perform the same function they do not help speed production. In a similar way, when we are trying to listen to two auditory messages at once we have problems in processing the information despite the fact that we have visual resources available. Sometimes alternative tools can help in manufacturing. A hand-held drill could help the manufacturing process if the powerful drill is being used but it will not be as efficient. In attention, sometimes other resources may help in performing a task, but not as efficiently as the specialised resource, and they will process information more slowly.

Evaluation of multiple resource theory

Like the module theory, the multiple resource theory provides a good explanation of the effect of task similarity in dual task experiments (e.g. Allport *et al.*, 1972). There are some neuropsychology studies that seem to support the notion of multiple resources. For example, Dawson and Schell (1982) carried out a study in which participants shadowed a message and were presented with a classically conditioned word in the non-attended ear. In the initial stage of the experiment (the conditioning phase) some words were paired with a mild electric shock. Subsequently any recognition of these words triggered an autonomic nervous system response. The words were presented in the non-attended ear, which for some participants was the right ear and for others the left ear. Dawson and Schell argue that the left and right cerebral hemispheres act as separate resources and that each is specialised for different processes. The right hemisphere seems to be capable of analysing speech but the left is specialised for speech reception and speech production. (Note also that information from the left ear is primarily analysed in the right hemisphere and information from the right ear is primarily analysed in the left hemisphere.) The results showed that there *was* an autonomic response to the unattended message in the left ear but *not* in the right ear. Payne and Wenger (1998) argue that it is difficult to explain these results with a single capacity model but a multiple resource model can account for the data. A single capacity model would predict that there would be a response in both ears or in neither. However, the multiple resource model predicts that, since the two hemispheres have different specialisation, the response to each ear will be different. In this case there is a response to the unattended message in the left ear, since this is processed by the right hemisphere which is able to analyse speech. There is no response to the unattended message in the right ear because this is processed by the left hemisphere. The left hemisphere is specialised for speech reception and production and, since the primary task is to shadow a message, this task takes priority (even though this information initially is sent to the right hemisphere). There are not enough resources to analyse the unattended message at the same time.

One of the problems of the multiple resource theory is the failure to specify the number of resources. Does multiple mean two, three or twenty? Also, as with the module model, there is no explanation of how the multiple resources work together. Our attentional processes are highly integrated but this model does not say how this is achieved.

Write a brief answer to the following:

1. What is the major factor that led to the development of the module/ multiple resource approach?
2. Explain the two problems that both the module and multiple resource theory share.

Progress exercise

Single or multiple processors?

Neither the single capacity models (e.g. Kahneman, Norman and Bobrow) nor the multiple capacity models (e.g. Allport, Navon and Gopher) seem to provide a complete explanation of divided attention. The major problem with the single capacity models is the failure to account for the effect of similarity in dual task studies. A major weakness of the multiple capacity models is that they do not explain how the separate parts of attention work together. Baddeley (1986) has proposed a **synthesis theory** which attempts to integrate the best features of both approaches. The synthesis theory combines a central, limited capacity processor (the central executive) with several modality-specific processing systems (the visuo-spatial sketchpad and the phonological loop). The central executive maintains overall control while the other systems deal with information that is relevant to them.

In a shadowing task listening and speaking would be processed by the phonological loop. Following a cursor on a screen would require the visuo-spatial sketchpad. The theory proposes that there is a general limit to attention capacity and that individual components also have limits. For example, trying to listen to two messages would overload our phonological loop but listening to a message and watching a screen would not.

Although this seems to be a good compromise which might help explain divided attention there are a few problems. One is that it is difficult to examine the role of the central executive. Another question about the theory is how the different components are integrated.

(This approach is discussed in detail in *Memory and Forgetting* (Henderson, 1999) as a theory of short-term memory, working memory. In a discussion of the theory Baddeley (1993) acknowledges that the ideas apply to both memory and attention but argues that working memory is the appropriate title to use.)

Summary

Divided attention is concerned with the ability to do two or more tasks at once and is studied using dual task experiments. These show that the ability to perform several tasks concurrently is influenced by a number of factors including task similarity, task difficulty and practice. Kahneman proposed that divided attention could be explained by a single, limited capacity central processor that allocated resources between tasks. Although this theory accounts for the effects of task difficulty and practice it does not explain why task similarity affects dual task performance. Norman and Bobrow suggested a modified version of a central capacity model in which tasks can be resource-limited or data-limited. This is a more flexible model but it has been described as non-falsifiable. Allport suggests that attentional processes use a number of modules which have individual resources (and therefore capacities). Different types of task would use different modules. This approach is much better at explaining the influence of task similarity and is supported by the findings of cognitive neuropsychology. However, the theory does not specify the number of modules used for attention nor how they are integrated. The multiple resource theory proposed by Navon and Gopher is similar to the modular approach and has comparable strengths and weaknesses.

The synthesis theory proposes that attention is controlled by both a central limited capacity processor (the central executive) and individual processors for different tasks.

Briefly describe the experiments of Spelke *et al.* (1976) and Allport *et al.* (1972). Then answer the following questions:

1. Which theory, Kahneman or Allport, explains the findings of Spelke *et al.* better?
2. Why is this theory better at explaining the results?
3. Which theory, Kahneman or Allport, explains the findings of Allport *et al.* better?
4. Why is this theory better at explaining the results?

Review exercise

Further reading

Allport, D.A. (1993) Attention and control. Have we been asking the wrong questions? A critical review of twenty-five years. In D.E. Meyer and S.M. Kornblum (eds) *Attention and Performance*, vol. XIV. London: MIT Press. This review of attention is complex but provides an excellent overview of the topic and is written by one of the foremost researchers in the field.

Payne, D.G. and Wenger, M.J. (1998) *Cognitive Psychology*. Boston: Houghton Mifflin. This cognitive psychology textbook is aimed at American undergraduates. It has a good section on divided attention in Chapter 5.

4

Automatic processing and action slips

Introduction

Evidence from dual task experiments and everyday experience shows that we are sometimes able to do two or more tasks at once. One important factor determining the ease with which we can do one, two or more tasks is practice. Tasks that initially require all our attention often become easier as we practise and eventually seem to require little or no mental effort. When learning to drive it initially seems an almost impossible task to co-ordinate the action of both feet with our hands, so changing gear requires intense concentration. An experienced driver, however, will change gear with little thought and may often be unaware that they have just changed gear. These types of observations have led to ideas about **automatic processing**. This is the notion that some tasks become so well practised that they make no demands on our attention processes. There is evidence that automatic processing can lead to failure in attention. The mistakes that result from attention failures are called **action slips**.

Automatic processing

Studies of divided attention have revealed that practice is one of the key factors in the performance of tasks. Some studies show that with practice participants are able to perform several complex tasks at once. One explanation of this is that practice reduces the amount of resources a task needs, and prolonged practice may result in tasks becoming 'automatic'. Posner and Snyder (1975) suggested that there was a difference between tasks that require conscious control and tasks that are activated solely as a result of past learning. Tasks that require no attention have been labelled automatic tasks and, as they do not need conscious control, they are said to use automatic processing. There are various ideas about automatic processing but most agree about the following features:

- Automatic processes are fast compared to processes requiring conscious control.
- Automatic processes are 'effortless' because there is no need to think about them.
- There is little or no awareness of automatic processes.
- Automatic processes are unavoidable since they are triggered by external or internal stimuli (rather than initiated consciously).

The **Stroop effect** is often used to demonstrate the nature of automatic processing and conscious control. This effect was first described by Stroop (1935) and is usually demonstrated by giving participants lists of words written in various coloured ink. The participants are instructed to name the *colour of the ink* for each word as quickly as they can. In Stroop's original study, in the control condition the list consisted of neutral non-colour-related words (e.g. chair, dog). Another list consisted of names of colours written in appropriate coloured ink (e.g. the word 'red' in red ink). This was the compatible condition. The third list consisted of names of colours written in inappropriate coloured ink (e.g. the word 'red' in green ink). This was the incompatible condition. The participants named the colour of the ink faster in the compatible condition than in the control condition. In the incompatible condition participants took longer to name the colour of the ink than in the control condition. One explanation is that naming the colour of the ink is an unfamiliar task and requires conscious control, but reading is so well practised for most adults that it has become automatic. Therefore in the third condition participants experience interference. As they try to name the colour of the ink (e.g. red) they have already read the word in the list (e.g. green). Try the variation of the Stroop effect in the progress exercise below. You should find that it takes longer to complete list two.

Shiffrin and Schneider's theory

Shiffrin and Schneider (1977) have proposed that there are two distinct ways of dealing with a task, one using controlled processing and the other using automatic processing. They claim that **controlled processes** require extensive attentional resources and are limited by capacity. These processes tend to be slow and involve a conscious effort. They are therefore flexible and can be adapted to meet different circumstances. Writing an essay is an example of using controlled processing. It requires a lot of resources and a person is consciously aware of attending to the task. The skill of essay-writing is not confined to one essay title but can be adapted to a variety of essays.

Automatic processes are not limited by capacity since they require no resources. They are fast and do not need conscious control. Automatic processes are therefore difficult to modify. An experienced driver would use automatic processing in an emergency stop. The sight of something in the road would trigger the reaction of stopping. They would not have to consciously attend to the task and deliberately press their left foot on the clutch and their right on the brake. However if the brake pedal was moved the driver would find driving difficult (driving would now require controlled processing). They would be unable to stop quickly and in an emergency would probably press the wrong pedal.

Schneider and Shiffrin (1977) investigated the nature of controlled and automatic processes using a visual search task (see Key research summary 2, p. 108). They used the task to study the factors that

Investigate the nature of automatic processing using a variation of the Stroop effect.

There are three font types in the following two lists: bold, italics and capitals. Your task is to name the type of font that each word is written in as fast as possible. For example, if you see the stimulus '**bold**' your response should be <u>bold</u>. However, if you see the stimulus '*bold*' your response should be <u>italics</u>. If you see the stimulus 'BOLD' your response should be <u>capitals</u>.

Compare how long it takes to read out the font types for list one and two.

List one	*List two*
bold	**capitals**
bold	**italics**
italics	*bold*
CAPITALS	BOLD
bold	**italics**
CAPITALS	ITALICS
bold	**capitals**
italics	*bold*
italics	*capitals*
CAPITALS	ITALICS
CAPITALS	BOLD
italics	*capitals*
bold	**capitals**
italics	*italics*
CAPITALS	BOLD
bold	**capitals**
CAPITALS	ITALICS
italics	*bold*
CAPITALS	BOLD
italics	*capitals*
bold	**italics**

Why did it take longer to name the fonts in list two?

(I would like to thank Hannah Lowe for demonstrating this variation of the Stroop effect to me.)

might affect the development of automaticity. In each of a series of experiments they asked participants to memorise a number of letters or numbers (the memory set). They were then shown a display of letters/numbers (called frames) and asked to decide whether any of the memory set appeared in the frame. They changed many variables such as the number of items in the memory set, the frame size and the speed of presentation. One important variable in the development of their theory was the kind of *mapping* used. In the **consistent mapping condition** only letters were used in the memory set and the distracter items in the frames were numbers. Participants therefore knew that if they saw a letter it was part of the memory set. In the **varied mapping condition** letters and numbers were used in the memory set and the frames were a mixture of letters and numbers. Participants had to search the frames to find the relevant characters.

The two mapping conditions produced very different results. The decision speed in the varied mapping condition was greatly affected by memory set size and frame size, whereas neither factor affected decision speed in the consistent mapping condition. Schneider and Shiffrin (1977) believe this is because controlled processing is used in the varied mapping condition, because each item has to be searched. However, in the consistent mapping condition automatic processing is used, because we have years of practice in distinguishing between numbers and letters. Furthermore, Shiffrin and Schneider (1977) found that after considerable practice there was improvement in a consistent mapping condition that consistently used some letters for the memory set and different letters as distracters. However, there was no such improvement in a varied mapping condition that used inconsistent letters in the memory set and as distracters. This was taken as evidence of the development of automaticity.

Evaluation

The series of experiments described by Schneider and Shiffrin (1977) seems to provide evidence of controlled and automatic processing, and Shiffrin and Schneider (1977) have demonstrated how automatic processes develop. The difference between varied and consistent mapping has been replicated a number of times (e.g. Fisk and Hodge, 1992) and seems to indicate that at least two processes are operating: controlled and automatic.

There are a variety of criticisms of Shiffrin and Schneider's theory. Eysenck and Keane (1995) claim that its greatest weakness is that it is descriptive rather than explanatory. The assertion that practice results in automatic processing merely points out what happens but it does not explain *how* it happens. Furthermore, there are a number of alternative explanations of the influence of practice. It could be that practice leads to faster processing of the task or that it changes the nature of the processes. Cheng (1985) favours the latter explanation and calls the use of a new method of processing 'restructuring'. For example, if you were to add two a hundred times it would be a time-consuming task $(2 + 2 + 2 + 2 + 2$ etc.), but if you realised that you could simply multiply two by a hundred it would be a much quicker process (2×100). You have not made the process of adding twos faster; you have restructured and found an alternative and more efficient way of processing the information. Cheng believes that Schneider and Shiffrin's results are explained better in terms of restructuring rather than automaticity.

Neuman (1984) is another critic of the Shiffrin and Schneider theory. He argues that many of the proposed criteria for automatic processing are rarely met. He claims that controlled and automatic processes merely represent different levels of control. 'Automatic' processes are controlled but are controlled below the level of conscious awareness. (Styles (1997) provides an excellent summary of Neuman's critique – see Further reading at the end of the chapter.)

Norman and Shallice's theory

Norman and Shallice (1986) have proposed an alternative theory of automaticity. They recognised that many tasks did not fit into the two categories of being either totally controlled or completely automatic. They suggested that there are three levels of processing:

- **Fully automatic processing** for tasks that require no conscious control.
- **Partially automatic processing** for tasks that do not need conscious control but which need monitoring. If several well-practised tasks are performed at once none of them needs conscious control but the progress of all the tasks needs to be checked (see contention scheduling, below).

- **Deliberate control** for difficult or unpractised tasks that require conscious control.

An important feature of the theory is that the three levels of processing require different types of control systems. Norman and Shallice argue that when several well-practised tasks are performed simultaneously we use partially automatic processing. The problem is that the tasks may interfere with each other. The type of control system needed here is **contention scheduling**. This is a system that allows the progress of each task to be monitored and arranged to avoid conflicts. For example, when you are preparing your breakfast there are a number of simple, well-practised tasks to perform: making a cup of coffee, preparing some toast and listening to the radio. None of these tasks requires much thought but there has to be some monitoring of the progress (scheduling) or you may end up with burnt toast and cold coffee. Difficult tasks require deliberate control and need a system of control that monitors every aspect in the performance of the task. Norman and Shallice labelled this the **supervisory attentional system**. You cannot read a book by concentrating on the page occasionally; you have to read each word and sentence in turn.

Evaluation

This approach is more flexible than the Shiffrin and Schneider theory since it suggests that there are several control systems. Eysenck and Keane (1995) claim that the Norman and Shallice approach is preferable 'because it provides a more natural explanation for the fact that some processes are fully automatic whereas others are only partially automatic'.

Although the Norman and Shallice theory is more flexible than Shiffrin and Schneider's, it still assumes that changes caused by practice are a result of automaticity. However, there are doubts about whether tasks are ever processed automatically. For example, Cheng (1985) believes that the changes caused by practice can be explained better by the concept of restructuring (see p. 46). Logan (1988) believes that the effects of practice are explained by changes in memory processes rather than automatic processing (see below).

Automaticity or memory? – the instance theory

Shiffrin and Schneider (1977) interpreted the results of their experiments on varied and consistent mapping as evidence of controlled and automatic processing. Logan (1988) has proposed a theory based on memory which provides an alternative explanation of the results (and of the effect of practice). One of the central assumptions of the theory is that each time a particular stimulus is encountered it is stored in memory as an instance, hence the name **instance theory**. Logan suggests that there are two ways participants can decide on a response in a task such as the visual search. The first is to use an *algorithm*. This is the use of a set of rules to make the decision and can be a relatively slow process. The second way is to use *memory retrieval*. When we have previously encountered a stimulus, we already have the memory of the correct response. In this case we can make the response based on memory rather than working through the rules. The more instances there are of the stimulus the quicker memory retrieval of the response becomes.

Logan's theory therefore suggests that an unpractised task is slow because we need to apply rules to perform it, but after prolonged practice tasks are performed quickly because the solution is stored in memory. A task may seem automatic because the stimulus triggers the retrieval of the appropriate response without the involvement of any other processes (we do not have to 'think about it'). Thus, according to Logan, 'automaticity is memory retrieval: performance is automatic when it is based on a single step direct access retrieval of past solutions from memory'.

Evaluation

The instance theory is useful in pointing out the importance of knowledge in performing a task. When we perform a task for the first time we do not necessarily lack resources, but we lack the knowledge of how to perform the task well. Practice may improve our performance because it increases our knowledge; we have more instances to use. Eysenck and Keane (1995) claim: 'Logan is probably right in his basic assumption that an understanding of automatic, expert performance will require detailed consideration of the knowledge acquired with practice, rather than simply the changes in processing which occur.'

The challenge facing cognitive psychologists now is to determine whether the changes caused by practice are due to changes in memory retrieval (Logan), changes in processing capacity (Shiffrin and Schneider), a restructuring of processing (Cheng), or a combination of factors.

Use the table below to compare the features of automatic processes and deliberate controlled processes.

Process	Automatic	Controlled
Speed		slow
Resources needed	little/none	
Awareness	not aware	

Progress exercise

Action slips

A lot of the mistakes that we make seem to be caused by failures of attention. Everyone will have experience of doing something they did not intend, such as brushing teeth with shaving cream. Sometimes our mistakes are caused by omission, such as putting boiling water into a teapot without the tea. These types of mistakes are known as **action slips**. Although some examples of action slips can be amusing, they can also be fatal. Many instances of driver or pilot error are the result of attentional failure and action slips. It is therefore important to understand the nature of action slips in order to avoid potential disasters. Before investigating the theories we need to look at what types of action slip occur.

Studies of action slips

Action slips are difficult to study accurately because by definition they are behaviours that were unintended. We do not know when or if an action slip will be made. If participants are asked to make mistakes then their behaviour becomes deliberate. Nevertheless there are two methods for investigating action slips: diary studies and laboratory studies.

Diary studies

Diary studies are a simple way of studying action slips and involve asking participants to keep a record of all the mistakes they make. For example, Reason (1979) asked 35 people to keep a diary of all the action slips they were aware of over a two-week period. The participants recorded a total of 433 action slips and Reason found that most of them could be classified into one of the following five categories:

1. The majority of slips (40 per cent) involved **storage failures**. These occur when actions or intentions are forgotten or recalled incorrectly. This leads to an action being repeated or omitted. For example, you might forget that you have added sugar to your tea and consequently add sugar twice. One of Reason's diarists started to walk home because he had forgotten that he had driven to work that day.

2. The next most common cause of slips (20 per cent) was **test failures**. These result from a failure to monitor the progress of an intended sequence and cause a switch to another action. For example, you might intend to have a cup of soup and put the kettle on but you make a cup of coffee instead.

3. A further 18 per cent of slips were classified as **sub-routine failures**. These are errors that involve the addition, or omission, of one stage in a sequence. For example, when making a cup of coffee you might forget to switch the kettle on and, despite performing all the other actions perfectly in the correct sequence, your coffee would be cold.

4. **Discrimination failures** accounted for 11 per cent of the slips. These involve a failure to discriminate between two objects. For example, you may mistake a carton of orange juice for a carton of milk and pour orange into your tea. I used to store chilli powder in a coffee jar until I made the mistake of making 'coffee' with chilli. Some discrimination failures can be temporal (a failure to recognise what time/day it is). For example, Reason quotes the case of someone who got up and dressed before realising that it was her day off.

5. **Programme assembly failures** only accounted for 5 per cent of the slips. These consist of an inappropriate combination of actions, such as unwrapping a sweet then throwing it away and putting the wrapper in your mouth. One of Reason's diarists habitually threw two dog biscuits to her dog and then put on her earrings before leaving for work. One morning she threw her earrings to the dog and found herself trying to attach a dog biscuit to her ear!

The diary studies give an interesting insight into the types of action slips that people make but there are several problems with the technique. First, the diary studies only record the mistakes that people are aware of or remember. There is no way of checking how many slips were undetected, or, more seriously, whether there is another type of mistake that has not been detected at all. Secondly, since these mistakes cannot be studied in detail, any of the categories identified by Reason may actually represent several different types of slip which just appear to be similar.

Laboratory studies

Laboratory-based studies of action slips use techniques which try to induce mistakes in participants. This is often achieved by creating a misleading context or expectation. For example, Reason (1992) asked participants to answer a series of questions as quickly as possible. The most common responses were one-word answers that all rhymed with 'oak'. For example:

Q: What sound does a frog make?
A: Croak
Q: What do we call a funny story?
A: Joke

The last question in this series was 'What do you call the white of an egg?' to which 85 per cent of the participants answered 'yolk' even though it was the wrong answer (the white of an egg is 'albumen'). The wrong answer had been induced in many participants because of the series of answers ending in an 'oak' sound. This had created the context and expectation of more 'oak'-like answers. When participants were

ATTENTION AND PATTERN RECOGNITION

only asked the last question, only 5 per cent answered 'yolk'. Many action slips have been produced in laboratory conditions, but it is not clear whether they bear much resemblance to natural action slips. In our everyday lives action slips occur when we are not 'thinking'; they happen when we are distracted or preoccupied. In laboratory studies participants are well motivated and typically have a desire to 'do well' and will therefore be concentrating on their behaviour.

The diary study technique records real mistakes that people have made but cannot provide an accurate record of all mistakes. Furthermore, it does not show how these mistakes were made. In contrast, the laboratory studies can provide an accurate record of the action slips made, but they are artificially induced and may not relate to the types of errors made in 'real life' (they lack **ecological validity**).

Progress exercise

Examine the following examples and, using Reason's categories on pp. 50–1, decide what type of action slip each example shows.

1. Putting the coffee jar in the fridge and the milk in the cupboard.

2. Getting a shirt out to wear and moments later getting another one.

3. 'Washing' your hair with conditioner.

4. Walking into the refectory when you intended to go to the library.

5. Putting an envelope in the post with no letter in it.

6. Telling a friend the same thing twice in the same conversation.

7. Driving to the wrong destination.

8. Throwing a letter away but holding the envelope.

9. Spraying hairspray onto your underarm.

10. Making an elaborate meal but failing to put the oven on.

52

Theories of action slips

Reason's theory

Reason (1992) suggests that behaviour is controlled in two different modes:

- an automatic mode which uses 'open loop' control. Open loop means an action is initiated but then is left to continue without feedback or supervision.
- a conscious control mode which is deliberate and uses 'closed loop' control. Closed loop control is used when an action is started and then monitored. Since there is constant feedback about the task it is a closed loop.

Closed loop, or conscious, control is slow and requires more effort, but since the action is monitored constantly responses are flexible and very few mistakes are made. Open loop, or automatic, control, on the other hand, is fast and allows attentional resources to be devoted to other tasks. The disadvantage of open loop control is that it is inflexible. Reason also believes that it is this type of control that leads to the vast majority of action slips because there is little or no feedback. In other words once we start an action using open loop control we no longer think about it. The progress of these automatic tasks may therefore be inappropriate.

Evaluation

The notion that action slips occur with automatic, highly practised tasks does seem to be consistent with the findings from Reason's diary study (1979). The five categories of action slip that Reason identified all seem to involve tasks that are not closely monitored. For example, if an action under automatic control is not monitored, part of it may be repeated leading to storage failures. Test failures may occur when an automatic action, which is common to several tasks, is performed. There is confusion about what the initial goal was since it is not monitored. When tasks are not monitored it is easy to pick one object instead of another, causing discrimination failures, etc.

There are a number of problems with this theory of action slips. First, there are now doubts about the concept of automatic processing (see p. 48). Logan (1988) has suggested that the characteristics attributed to automatic processing can be explained by memory retrieval. This raises the question: are action slips a failure of processing or a failure of memory? The second problem stems from the idea that it is only automatic control of well-practised tasks that leads to action slips. This seems to oversimplify the topic. Although the majority of mistakes occur when using automatic control, there may be other factors involved. For example, the nature of the tasks may influence the probability of mistakes. Making a pot of tea can be a well-practised task, but it is not very important and we are liable to make mistakes. An experienced skydiver may be well practised at jumping from an aeroplane, but the action is potentially life-threatening and so it is unlikely that action slips will occur. Gymnasts practise an action time after time to *prevent* any mistakes. A final problem is that the theory does not explain why action slips occur when closed loop, or conscious, control is used. Healy (1976) asked participants to circle all the letter 't's in a passage. This requires conscious control yet most of the participants failed to circle the 't' in 'the'.

Sellen and Norman's theory

Sellen and Norman (1992) have proposed that actions are governed by **schemas** which are organised in hierarchies (schemas are chunks of knowledge of how to deal with the world). The schemas at the highest level are called parent schemas and these are concerned with overall intentions, such as making a cup of coffee. Lower-level schemas are called child schemas and they correspond to the individual actions needed to accomplish the parent schemas, such as putting the kettle on, getting a cup, putting coffee in the cup, etc. Schemas trigger actions when there is an appropriate level of activation. The activation level of schemas is determined by intentions (e.g. I want a cup of coffee) and the environmental stimuli (e.g. when the kettle boils it triggers the action of pouring water into the cup).

This model proposes that action slips can occur when there are errors in the activation of either parent or child schema. This can occur in a number of ways:

- Errors in the formation of an intention. These result in the wrong parent schema being activated (e.g. you might intend to drive to the shop but find that you have driven to work instead).

- Activation of the wrong child schema (e.g. you put coffee in the teapot instead of your cup).
- A child schema is not activated (e.g. you forget to switch the kettle on).
- Faulty triggering of active schemas so that an action is taken over by the wrong parent schema (e.g. you are searching the internet for useful psychology sites, but suddenly you realise that you have spent the last ten minutes looking at sites about your favourite television programme).

Evaluation

As with Reason's theory, this approach seems to provide a good explanation of the results from Reason's diary study. For example, if child schemas are repeated this would cause storage failures; if there are problems in the formation of an intention a test failure would happen, etc.

This theory does not adequately explain why action slips occur when a task is being processed with deliberate control. It also seems to assume that action slips occur when using automatic processing. However, as we have seen (p. 48), there are doubts about the nature of automatic processing.

Applying theories of action slips

Diary studies of action slips (e.g. Reason, 1979) seem to indicate that slips and errors are a fairly common part of our lives. Most of the time these slips are trivial and easily remedied; however, in some circumstances these types of slips can have disastrous consequences. When people are driving a car, piloting an aircraft or operating complicated machinery there is little time to recognise that a slip or error has occurred and then to correct the fault. Reason (1979) examined a number of British civil aircraft accidents and found that most instances of pilot error involved action slips rather than an error of judgement. A significant proportion of these errors occurred when the crew were dealing with a genuine emergency such as an engine failure. The emergency itself was rarely sufficient to cause a crash but captured the pilots' attention. This created the conditions where inappropriate actions could occur (the pilots were distracted). For example, a number of accidents involving twin-engine light aircraft occurred after developing problems with one engine. The pilots responded promptly to the emergency but switched off the healthy engine rather than the failing engine. The challenge facing psychologists is to find ways of helping design engineers, managers and training instructors to prevent such accidents.

One problem psychologists have in studying accidents is that there is rarely one cause. Inquiries and studies of major accidents usually reveal a mixture of individual mistakes, inappropriate rules/plans and corporate failure. In his book *Human Error*, Reason (1990) has proposed a conceptual framework of how accidents occur, called the generic error modelling system (GEMS). He suggests there are three basic error types:

1. Skill-based slips (and lapses) – these are the slips individuals make because of execution or storage failures (see types of action slips on p. 50).
2. Rule-based mistakes – these occur when the action is as planned but the plan is wrong. This may happen if the rules governing the actions are poor or good rules are misapplied.
3. Knowledge-based mistakes – these occur when plans go wrong because of previous knowledge or experience. This may happen when a person is overconfident and does not apply or check plans/ rules or selects the wrong response to a situation.

In a review of accidents at nuclear power plants Reason found that one or more of these factors were always involved. For example, in 1979 an operator at the Oyster Creek power station intended to close two pump discharge valves (A and E) but accidentally switched off four (A and E plus B and C). This caused all circulation to the reactor core to be shut off. This is an example of an action slip leading to a dangerous situation. However, most major accidents are not caused by one or other of these types of error but by a combination of them. For example, the explosion at the Chernobyl nuclear power station in 1986 was due to a complex sequence of slips and mistakes. During test procedures an operator error led to reactor power being reduced to less than 10 per cent. The operating team carried on with the test program even though the safety procedures prohibited the operation at less than 20 per cent capacity. There were then further safety procedure violations before an explosion within the core blew off the 1,000 tonne concrete cap.

Reason concludes that it is impossible to devise any system that can guarantee to eliminate all errors or mistakes ('to err is human'). He argues that the only way to combat the problem of human error in high-risk technologies is to try to mitigate the consequences. For example, designers of machines should build-in system responses to error. These can be in the form of: warnings (to alert operators that a mistake has been made); locking (to prevent further use until the error has been corrected); 'do nothing' (not responding until the correct response has been made); self-correction; dialogue (asking whether the proposed action is the correct one); or teaching (showing the machine a new correct action). However, the problem with 'fail safe' mechanisms, as a number of inquiries into major accidents have shown, is that they can be switched off or overridden. Reason suggests that another way of reducing the impact of errors is to build-in procedures or mechanisms so that other people detect them.

Robertson, Manly and their colleagues at the Applied Psychology Unit at Cambridge have investigated 'absentmindedness' or attention failures in both brain-injured patients and healthy control participants (Robertson *et al.*, 1997a; Manly *et al.*, 1999). They have devised a method of testing lapses of attention which they have called the sustained attention to response test (SART). This is a simple test in which a random series of digits from 1 to 9 are presented at regular intervals on a screen. The participants' task is to press a button after each number is presented *except* when the number 3 occurs. This apparently simple task becomes more difficult over time and few participants last more than four minutes before pressing the button after a number 3 is presented. Most participants respond to the number 3 many times in four minutes. Robertson suggests that this is because participants drift from controlled processing into automatic processing and this creates the conditions that produce action slips. This is supported by the finding that reaction times immediately preceding the incorrect responses became significantly shorter (suggesting that participants were no longer concentrating on the task – it was becoming automatic).

Robertson *et al*. (1997a) found a significant correlation between the scores on SART and action slips in everyday life in both the brain-injured patients and the healthy control participants. This suggests that the score on SART can be used to predict 'absentmindedness' in participants. Robertson and Manly have also found that warning participants that their response time was getting faster (i.e. that they were likely to make an error) prevented action slips. These findings suggest that there are a number of practical uses of SART. First, it can be used to test potential rehabilitation regimes that have been devised to aid in the recovery from brain injury. There is evidence that improving performance on attention tasks can aid recovery of general cognitive abilities following brain injury (Robertson *et al.*, 1997b). Secondly, it can be used to train people to improve their performance on attentional tasks. Robertson and Manly found that a training program which warned participants of potential errors improved subsequent scores on SART. If this effect transfers to 'real-life' tasks then this technique could help train people who are required to use sustained attention in their jobs (for example, in air traffic control).

Summary

Prolonged practice of some tasks seems to change the way they are processed. Shiffrin and Schneider have proposed that there are two ways of dealing with a task, controlled processing and automatic processing. Controlled processes require conscious control of the task; they tend to be slow and require effort. Automatic processes are fast and, since they do not require conscious control, demand no effort. Although this idea was supported by an elegant series of experiments, it seems to describe the process of automaticity rather than explain it. Norman and Shallice suggested an alternative theory which proposed three levels of processing: fully automatic, partially automatic and deliberate control, all of which require different types of control systems. This approach is more flexible than Shiffrin and Schneider's, but still does not explain the nature of automaticity. Logan claimed that all the studies that point to automatic processing can be explained in terms of memory retrieval. Reason studied both natural errors, using a diary method, and mistakes induced in laboratories. He found that action slips could largely be grouped into five categories and claimed that they occur as a result of automatic processing and a lack of monitoring of well-practised tasks. Sellen and Norman argued that actions are governed by a hierarchy of schemas. Action slips are a result of inappropriate triggering of parent or child schemas. However, neither theory explains why errors occur when using deliberate control. Action slips are a contributory factor in many accidents. Reason has argued that, since some degree of error is inevitable with human operators, the effects of action slips can only be reduced by identifying and dealing with them.

Answer the following:

1. What are the features of automatic processing?
2. What are the alternative ideas that seek to explain the effect of practice?
3. What is the link between automatic processing and action slips?

Review exercise

Further reading

Eysenck, M.W. and Keane, M.T. (1995) *Cognitive Psychology – A Student's Handbook* (3rd edn). Hove, UK: Lawrence Erlbaum Associates Ltd. The end of Chapter 5 has a very good discussion of automatic processing and action slips.

Styles, E.A. (1997) *The Psychology of Attention*. Hove, UK: Psychology Press. This book is not aimed at A level standard and can be difficult to understand at first. However, it does have a very detailed discussion of automatic processing in Chapter 8.

Pattern recognition

Introduction

Examine the following set of characters and decide which one is different:

T *T*T ᴛ ᴛ **T** ᴛ A ᴛ *T*

Did you decide that the character third from the right was different? If you inspect the line carefully you will realise that *all* the characters are different. However, we tend to perceive the line of characters as being one 'A' and nine 'T's. There is something about nine of the characters that we recognise as a T even though they are all different. There are hundreds of different fonts used in books yet we are able to recognise letters in a fraction of a second and read the words accurately. Everyone's handwriting is different but what initially seems to be a meaningless scrawl becomes recognisable as letters. Recognition of letters and reading are skills we barely think about as adults, but it is a complicated process.

Pattern recognition has been defined as 'the ability to abstract and integrate certain elements of a stimulus into an organised scheme for memory storage and retrieval' (Solso, 1998). Pattern recognition is central to perception and attention and involves an interaction between sensation, perception, short-term memory and long-term memory.

Features of pattern recognition

Solso (1998) has outlined five principles of pattern recognition, which are based both on laboratory studies and on everyday experiences. He points out that pattern recognition enables us to:

- Recognise familiar patterns quickly and accurately. We recognise letters without effort and can easily pick out pictures of our house, friends, etc.
- Recognise and classify unfamiliar objects. No matter how unique a font is we are able to analyse letters. If you visit Greece you will encounter new letters but within a few days these become easy to recognise.
- Accurately recognise shapes and objects from different angles. The appearance of a cube varies when viewed from different angles but it is still recognised as a cube.
- Accurately identify patterns and objects even when partly hidden. A square partially hidden by a triangle is recognised as a square. A person sitting behind a desk is still recognised as a person even though you can only see half of them.
- Recognise patterns quickly, with ease, and with automaticity. The images reaching our eyes are constantly changing in shape, size and brightness but we are able to process this information rapidly and with no apparent effort.

There are a number of theories of how pattern recognition is achieved:

- **Template matching theories** suggest that patterns are recognised when the incoming sensory stimuli are matched with a template, or copy, of the pattern in long-term memory.

- **Feature analysis** involves analysing the sensory stimuli into simple features. Feature detection theories propose that any pattern is a combination of these features and pattern recognition is the identification of the combination.
- **Prototype theories** suggest that pattern recognition consists of comparing sensory stimuli against an idealised mental form, or prototype, of the pattern.

Although there are differences in approach, at a basic level all theories agree that pattern recognition involves a matching process between the visual stimulus and information from memory.

Top-down and bottom-up processing

An examination of the theories of pattern recognition raises the question of whether pattern recognition involves **top-down** or **bottom-up** processing. The argument about top-down or bottom-up is one of the central debates in perception and attention. Top-down theories argue that pattern recognition starts with a hypothesis about the pattern as a whole and this leads to identification and also recognition of the components. This top-down approach is illustrated well in the recognition of ambiguous stimuli such as the Necker cube (Figure 5.1). This can be perceived in two ways: the shaded face can appear to come out of the page or go into the page. The information about this figure is limited and perception depends on which 'hypothesis' (in or out) is accepted. The components of the cube can be perceived, but only as part of a whole. Top-down theories also stress the importance of context and expectation (see p. 75).

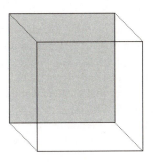

Figure 5.1 A Necker cube

Bottom-up theories argue that pattern recognition starts with the identification of components which are then grouped together to enable the recognition of the whole. For example, this approach argues that the recognition of a simple letter like N has to start with the analysis of the individual components: |, \, and |. These components can then be combined so that the letter N can be recognised. As each letter is recognised they can then be combined to form a word. Thus recognition starts at the bottom with the individual features and builds up.

Template matching theories

The template matching theories assume that pattern recognition occurs when external stimuli are matched with an internal template of the pattern. One way to imagine the templates is to think of them as a mental stencil. If a visual stimulus fits the stencil or template, it is recognised. For example, in Figure 5.2 the A on the left represents a letter you might see on a page. This 'fits' the internal template shown on the right and, since the two match, the pattern can be recognised.

Figure 5.2 **Template matching theory. The stimulus 'fits' the template**

This theory of pattern recognition assumes that vast numbers of templates are stored. We might therefore have a large number of templates for recognising each letter and number. Another assumption is that templates are created by experiences. For example, if you were to visit Russia you would see many letters that did not fit any of your templates and they would be difficult to recognise. However, within a few days of looking at maps, shop signs, etc. the new letters appear familiar and recognisable. The template theory suggests that this is because new templates have been formed.

There is general agreement that pattern recognition must at some level involve a match between the stimulus and some internal form. Solso (1998) points out that patterns and objects need to be recognised as matching a long-term memory. This is exactly what the template matching hypothesis proposes. An external stimulus is matched against an internal template and pattern recognition occurs. Template matching works well in computer systems where an exact match between a stimulus and a template can be made (e.g. barcodes or numbers printed on cheques).

The fundamental problem of a template matching theory is that recognition only occurs when there is a one-to-one match between the stimulus and the template. Payne and Wenger (1998) point out that a slight distortion of shape, size or orientation would cause a mismatch (see Figure 5.3).

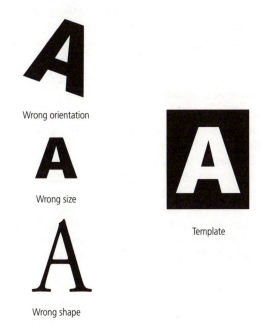

Figure 5.3 **Template matching theory. The effect of changing the stimulus pattern**

Each variation of a pattern would therefore need a separate template, each matching the precise pattern. Pattern recognition would require millions of separate templates. Even the recognition of one letter would require thousands of templates. This raises the question of where all these templates are stored. As Solso (1998) has noted, 'If we were to store that many templates, our cerebrum would be so bulky we would need a wheelbarrow to cart it'! Another problem with this theory is that pattern recognition would be a very slow process if we had to match every stimulus with one of millions of templates. However, pattern recognition occurs very rapidly. For example, the average reader typically reads about 250 words per minute. This means we recognise about 1,000 to 1,500 letters a minute. There is doubt whether this feat could be achieved if each letter had to be matched with millions of potential templates.

A final problem of the template matching theory is that it does not explain the ability to recognise new variations of a pattern (Solso, 1998). Novel versions of letters appear in advertising all the time but we are able to recognise them immediately. The template theory could only explain this by suggesting that new templates are formed almost instantaneously.

Geons – an alternative to templates?

The problems of the template theory could be summarised by the claim that the theory is too 'rigid'. Templates are not flexible enough to recognise alternative versions of the same pattern. Biederman (1987) has proposed a much more flexible model which is based on **geons** (which stands for geometric ions). This model suggests there are a limited number of simple geometric shapes, or geons, which are used in the analysis of complex shapes. Any pattern, shape or object can be broken down into the component geons. For example, a mug consists of a cylinder with an ellipse on the side (the handle). If the same two geons are combined differently, with the ellipse on top of the cylinder, they create a bucket (see Figure 5.4).

Biederman argues that pattern and object recognition consists of *recognition by components*, in which complex forms are identified by their component geons. Biederman and his colleagues have identified twenty-four geons which could potentially create an astronomical number of shapes (for example, just three geons arranged in all possible ways could produce 1.4 billion objects).

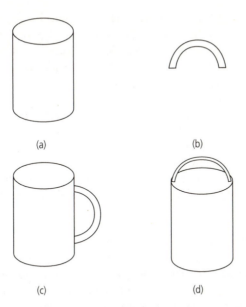

(a)

(b)

(c)

(d)

Figure 5.4 **Shape recognition using geons. Shape (a) can be combined with shape (b) to form a mug (c) or a bucket (d) (based on Biederman, 1987)**

The geon theory shares some of the features of a template matching model but it also has some of the characteristics of feature detection theories, which are discussed below.

Describe three ways in which the letter **P** could be changed so that it did not fit into the template **P**

Progress exercise

Feature detection theories

Feature detection theories propose that patterns are recognised by analysis of the individual features of the pattern. As each simple feature is analysed and detected it can be added to the others to build a complete representation of the pattern. This is a bottom-up process in which first the features are detected and then the pattern or object is recognised. For example, this theory would suggest that the sight of a word such as MANGO does not immediately conjure up an image of a tropical fruit. The word has to be analysed in stages, and the first stage is to analyse the features of each letter. The first letter has the features |, \, / and | and could be recognised as an M, the second has the features /, - and \ and is an A, etc.

Selfridge's **pandemonium model** is a good example of the feature detection approach. Selfridge (1959) suggested that there are four stages of pattern recognition and that 'demons' perform specific tasks at each stage (see Figure 5.5).

The first stage of analysis of a pattern, such as the M in the diagram, is to record the image that falls onto the retina. This is the responsibility of the *image demons* who then pass the information to the *feature demons* for the next stage. The feature demons analyse the image for specific features such as vertical lines, horizontal lines, curves, angles, etc. Each line, angle or curve has its own feature demon (i.e. there will be a '/' demon and a '⌐' demon and so on). If a feature demon detects the presence of its feature, it passes the information to the next stage, the *cognitive demons*. Each cognitive demon is responsible for detecting one pattern (thus 26 cognitive demons are needed to recognise upper-case letters and 26 are needed for lower-case). This pattern is detected by the presence of the individual features. However, many letters share similar features and feature demons will alert a number of cognitive demons. The letters N and M, for example, share the features |, \ and |. The final task of recognition is left to the *decision demon*. As the cognitive demons are alerted they begin to shout at the decision demon (in effect shouting 'It's me'). The analogy of many cognitive demons shouting for recognition suggests **pandemonium**, hence the title of the model. However, one cognitive demon will shout loudest because it will have the most features. For example, N and M share many features but an N does not have a / nor a ∨ feature so the M demon will shout loudest at the decision demon and an M will be recognised.

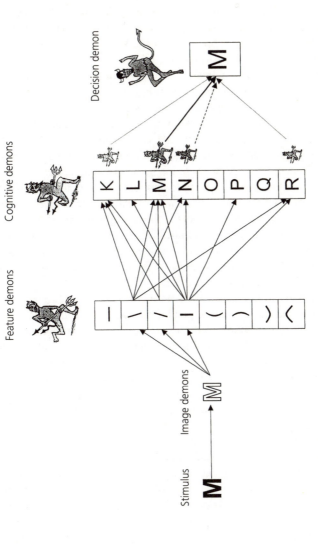

Figure 5.5 The pandemonium model (based on Selfridge, 1959)

The biology of feature detection

There is strong support for the feature detection theory from neuro-physiological studies. These are studies which investigate the responses of individual cells in the brain. Hubel and Wiesel (1959, 1965, 1968) and Hubel (1963) have performed a number of studies of the visual cortex in both cats and monkeys (see Key research study 3 on p. 110). They presented various visual stimuli to the animals and recorded the neural activity of single cells in the visual cortex. They found three types of cell which responded to differing levels of complexity of the stimulus: simple cells, complex cells, and hypercomplex cells.

The **simple cells** only respond to stimuli that are in a particular orientation and in a specific location in the visual field. For example, a simple cell may only respond to horizontal lines in the right lower corner of the visual field. If a line was vertical or at 45 degrees the cell would not respond even if it was in the appropriate part of the visual field. A horizontal line would not trigger a response if it were in a different part of the visual field. The **complex cells** respond to lines and edges of a particular orientation regardless of where they appear in the visual field. A complex cell that is sensitive to horizontal lines will respond to horizontal lines no matter where the line appears. However, the cell will not respond if the line or edge changes orientation. The **hypercomplex cells** also respond to lines but are sensitive to length and angles. Some hypercomplex cells respond best to combinations of lines and complex features. So whereas complex cells respond to lines of particular orientations, such as /, \ and –, hyper-complex cells respond to combinations of features, such as A. There is also evidence of hypercomplex cells that respond to complex stimuli such as hands and faces. For example, Perrett *et al*. (1990) found a hypercomplex cell that responded to faces. Furthermore, the cell responded best to faces in which the eyes pointed in a specific direction!

This neurophysiological evidence seems to lend considerable support for the feature detection theories. The action of the various types of cell in the visual cortex seems to be a physiological description of feature detection theory. However, there are problems with the neurophysiological data. First, some researchers have questioned the existence of hypercomplex cells (e.g. Bruce *et al*., 1996). Secondly, if hypercomplex cells do exist there is a question of how specialised they need to be. If we were to need a cell to recognise every face from every angle, and cells for every conceivable shape, we would run out of cells (Payne and Wenger, 1998). As Mollon (1982) pointed out, 'It would be no good having a system in which there were, say, single units specific to chartreuse-coloured Volkswagens moving left at a distance of ten metres.'

Evaluation

Apart from the neurophysiological evidence there are a variety of factors that support the feature detection theories. The feature detection models provide a much more flexible account of pattern recognition than template matching theories. For example, all letter 'A's share the same basic features of /, – and \. Detection of these features allows recognition of an A regardless of size, shape or orientation of the letter. The feature detection approach is also supported by psychological evidence. For example, Neisser (1964) tested the feature detection theory by using visual search studies. He presented participants with a block of letters and asked them to find a target letter as quickly as possible. He found that the time taken was strongly influenced by the level of similarity of the features of the target and distracter letters. The detection of the target was slower when the distracter letters had similar features to the target than when the features were dissimilar. For example, if the target letter is M it is difficult to detect amongst distracter letters such as N, H, or V. The letter M is detected much faster if the distracter letters are O, Q, or G. This suggests recognition involves analysis of features. When letters share features it requires more time to eliminate distracters.

The feature detection theories provide a bottom-up explanation of pattern recognition. One problem with this is that the theories fail to account for the effects of context and expectations. An ambiguous pattern can be perceived differently in different contexts yet it always has the same features. For example, in Figure 5.6 (p. 76) the central character can be seen as a letter B if one reads across the page, but as a number 13 if one reads down the page. This is more consistent with a top-down explanation of pattern recognition. Feature detection theories suggest that words are recognised by analysing the individual features of each letter. However, when Healy (1976) asked participants to circle all the 't's in a passage they tended to miss the 't's in 'the'. Healy suggests that this is because 'the' is processed as a unit rather than by individual features. Further doubt about the bottom-up approach is provided by some image stabilisation studies. Image stabilisation on the retina results in a fading of the image. Inhoff and Topolski (1994) found that when they presented participants with stabilised images of compound words like teacup or eyebrow the image did not fade in a random fashion. The images tended to fade leaving meaningful fragments such as 'cup' or 'eye' rather than non-meaningful fragments such as 'eac' or 'ebr'. Payne and Wenger (1998) point out that this seems inconsistent with a feature detection model and appears to show the influence of the knowledge of word meaning, or the influence of top-down processing.

Our experiences and experimental evidence show that patterns (and objects) can be recognised even when some features are obscured. Eysenck and Keane (1995) point out that the feature detection models have problems in explaining this. If patterns are recognised by analysing their component features, how can we recognise them when one or more of these features is hidden from view? Another problem of the feature detection theory is that features are not the only factor in pattern recognition – it is the relationship between the features that is important. For example, the features | and – appear in both T and L. The key to recognising whether a letter is a T or an L is the relationship between the features.

The feature detection models do not seem to provide a complete explanation of pattern recognition. Yet despite the problems of the theories some form of feature analysis does appear to take place. The neurophysiological data suggest that analysing the simple features of patterns is a fundamental aspect of pattern recognition. Solso (1998) has suggested that feature analysis is a stage that must take place before a higher level of pattern analysis can occur.

Progress exercise

Write brief answers to the following questions:

1. How would the feature detection model explain the recognition of the letter K?
2. What three types of cells in the visual cortex would respond to the letter K?
3. If the letter K was placed in either a list of 'O's, 'Q's and 'C's or in a list of 'V's, 'X's and 'Y's, in which list would it be easier to detect it?
4. Why does this support the feature detection theory?

Prototype theories

Prototype theories suggest that pattern recognition occurs by matching external stimuli with an idealised abstraction of a pattern, a prototype. Prototypes are the typical patterns that are stored in long-term memory and represent the best representation of a pattern. This theory suggests we have *one* prototype of, for example, a letter R. We would compare all other 'R's, including new versions, against this idealised version. If there is a match then the letter is recognised; if there is a mismatch then the pattern would be compared to another prototype.

Solso (1998) identifies two theoretical models of prototype formation: the **central-tendency model** and the **attribute-frequency model**. The central-tendency model suggests that a prototype represents the average from a set of exemplars (i.e. if the attributes of the examples could be assigned a numerical value the prototype would be the *mean* value). In the attribute-frequency model a prototype is seen as representing the most common combination of features or attributes (i.e. the prototype is the *mode* value of the attributes).

Evaluation

The prototype theories are a much more 'economical' way of explaining a matching process than the template theories (Solso, 1998). Instead of storing thousands of templates for each pattern, such as a letter, one prototype would be needed. The notion that patterns are matched against one prototype rather than thousands of templates per letter seems to explain the speed of recognition of letters, words and patterns. This approach is more flexible than the template theories and can explain the recognition of novel stimuli better. Novel stimuli can be matched against various prototypes to find which is the best fit.

One of the problems of the prototype theories is that they do not explain the effect of context (Eysenck, 1993). For example, the image in Figure 5.7(a) (p. 77) can be seen as the face of an old woman or the face of a young woman depending on the context in which it is shown. However, the character should correspond to one prototype regardless of context. Another problem has been identified by Solso (1998) who questions whether matching has to be a more exact process than the prototype theories suggest. For example, prototypes of a B, R and P would be very similar. Therefore, when reading different fonts or handwriting it should be easy to confuse one with the other, yet we seldom make mistakes in letter or pattern recognition. The lack of mistakes suggests a more exact match is made.

Prototype theories are often described as being more 'flexible' than template theories. Briefly explain what is meant by flexible and discuss one benefit and one problem of this flexibility.

Pattern recognition: an integrated view

There seems to be some evidence for all of the theories of pattern recognition yet none of them provides a complete explanation. One possible reason for this is that each theory may be essentially correct but is an explanation of only one stage of a complicated process. Solso (1998) has suggested that a coherent picture of pattern recognition only emerges if one takes an **integrated view** of the theories. At a simple level, patterns can only be recognised when the elements, or features, of the pattern are detected. There is both psychological and neurophysiological evidence that feature detection takes place. However, feature detection does not appear to offer a comprehensive account of pattern recognition and fails to explain how features are combined. The template theory offers a better explanation of how combinations of features are recognised for simple patterns. However, this theory has problems in explaining how so many different variations of a pattern can be recognised, or how several complex patterns can be recognised as the same class of object. The prototype theory seems to account for the ability to recognise complex patterns as belonging to the same class of object (for example, an office chair and a dining-room chair are both recognised as 'chairs' even though they only share some features). However, complex patterns cannot be recognised if their individual features have not been analysed. Thus any theory seems to account for only one facet of pattern recognition. In an examination of pattern (or form) recognition, Solso (1998) concluded:

The many theories of form perception are complementary rather than antagonistic. Form perception is a complicated affair, and, at present, no single comprehensive theory has been developed to account for all of its components.

The notion that pattern recognition involves a number of stages of processing, which might involve feature detection at one stage, proto-type matching at another, etc., is supported by evidence from cognitive neuropsychology. Ellis and Young (1989) have studied various types of *visual agnosia*. These are impairments of perceptual recognition that are caused by damage to the brain. Some forms of agnosia seem to damage the early stage of visual processing so that, although an individual can detect light, colour and movement, they cannot perceive shapes. In other forms of agnosia individuals can perceive shapes (they can, for example, draw objects they have seen) but cannot recognise them. Ellis and Young (1989) have concluded that object recognition involves a number of stages including initial representation, viewer-centred representation and object recognition units.

The role of context and expectations in pattern recognition

One problem with all of the theories of pattern recognition is that they do not explain the role of context or expectations. However, a variety of examples show that recognition is influenced by both factors. One of the best demonstrations of the effect of context is shown in Figure 5.6. The central character is perceived as a B or a 13 depending on whether it is read in a series of letters (across the page) or a series of numbers (down the page). However, the stimulus remains the same and has the same features. All of the theories of pattern recognition examined in this chapter predict that the character would always be perceived as the same letter or number.

The effect of context on letter recognition is demonstrated experi-mentally in the **word superiority effect**. This is the finding that letters can be identified faster and more accurately if they appear in the context of a word than if they are in a random set of letters or presented alone. For example, Wheeler (1970) briefly presented participants with a letter (such as D) and then with two letters (D and G). Participants were asked to determine which of the two letters had been presented initially.

Figure 5.6 **The effect of context**

Wheeler then used exactly the same procedure with words, so that after a brief presentation of the word 'WIND' participants were shown 'WIND' and 'WING'. Recognition was better in the word condition.

Expectation also plays a role in the recognition and perception of patterns and objects. We sometimes perceive what we expect to see or were primed to see. For example, Leeper (1935) found that the perception of an ambiguous face (Figure 5.7(a)) can be influenced by prior presentation of a similar unambiguous face. If the 'young woman' (Figure 5.7(b)) is presented before the ambiguous figure, the latter tends to be perceived as a young woman. However, if the 'old woman' (Figure 5.7(c)) is shown first, the ambiguous figure is perceived as an old woman.

The influence of context and experience seems to be explained better by top-down theories of perception. These emphasise the role of past experience and knowledge in recognition of patterns and objects.

Summary

Pattern recognition is the ability to pick out and organise some stimuli which can then be identified from long-term memory. There are a number of theories of how this recognition process occurs. The template matching theories suggest that pattern recognition takes place when a stimulus is matched against a mental representation of a pattern (a template). Despite their intuitive appeal these theories have problems

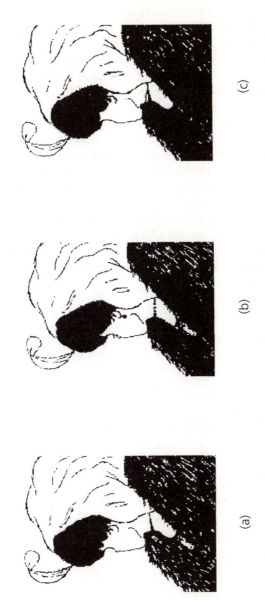

Figure 5.7 Ambiguous figure. From *Psychology, Fifth Edition* by Henry Gleitman, Alan J. Fridlund, Daniel Reisberg. Copyright © 1999, 1995, 1991, 1986, 1981 by W.W. Norton & Company, Inc. Used by permission of W.W. Norton & Company, Inc.

(a)   (b)   (c)

in explaining how the many variations of a pattern can be recognised. Templates are not flexible and a separate template would be needed for each slight variation in a pattern. Feature detection theories propose that patterns are recognised by analysing the individual features of the pattern. These theories have received support from both behavioural and neurophysiological studies. Studies of cells in the visual cortex suggest that feature detection does take place. However, feature detection theories have problems in explaining the effect of context and expectation. Prototype theories suggest that patterns are recognised by matching a stimulus against an idealised version of the pattern (a prototype). This is a flexible approach to pattern recognition but it does not account for the effect of context. The flexibility of the theory does not seem to explain the accuracy of pattern recognition. Solso (1998) has proposed that each of the theories of pattern recognition may be essentially correct but may be describing a different stage of the process. All of the theories of pattern recognition are bottom-up theories and do not explain the influence of expectation and context. These factors are better explained by top-down theories of perception.

Review exercise

Briefly outline how the template, feature detection and prototype theories would explain the recognition of the letter A. Discuss the main problem of each theory.

Further reading

Solso, R.L. (1998) *Cognitive Psychology* (5th edn). Boston: Allyn and Bacon. This is a good textbook on cognitive psychology which is aimed at American undergraduates. It is written in a clear style and Chapter 4 provides an interesting and informative discussion of pattern recognition.

Payne, D.G. and Wenger, M.J. (1998) *Cognitive Psychology*. Boston: Houghton Mifflin. This is another advanced textbook but again it is very clear. Chapter 4 has a good section on pattern recognition which takes a slightly different perspective from that of Solso.

6

Face recognition

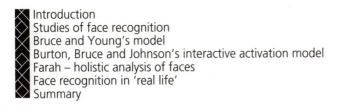
Introduction

In an average day you may see hundreds of faces. Some are familiar and instantly identifiable faces, such as family and friends. Some faces will be familiar but will evoke little more than a name, such as some of the people in your psychology class. Other faces will be recognisable but anonymous, such as people who live at the far end of the street. We can also easily recognise unfamiliar faces – for example, you notice when a person who gets served in front of you in the newsagent gets on the same bus as you. We can even recognise if pictures of a face taken from several angles are of the same person.

We seem to have an extraordinary ability to recognise faces. We can spot a friend in a football crowd even though their face is a small feature amongst thousands. We can recognise someone years after last seeing him or her even though their face has changed with age. Yet all faces comprise essentially the same basic features. Faces have a mouth, a nose, eyes, ears and, usually, hair. Despite the apparent uniformity of faces we can distinguish between them with ease.

Faces also have an important social role and have a special significance in our lives. We use faces as our primary means of identification. If you talk with someone about a mutual friend you usually have a mental image of his or her face. A face represents a person. So, for example, if there are pictures of staff at the entrance to the Psychology department, they will be pictures of the staff's *faces*, not of, say, their feet (many people keep a photograph of a loved one's face in their wallet/purse; few keep pictures of feet!). Faces are used in a social context and are used to communicate. Hearing someone talk on the telephone does not convey as much information as seeing someone talk. One of the reasons for this is that faces also convey information about emotions. Even simple cartoon pictures of a face can depict happiness, sadness, surprise, etc. which can be universally recognised.

There has been a great deal of research into face recognition but until the late 1970s much of this research was concentrated on one or other variable, such as age, sex, memory interval, etc. A new approach emerged in the 1980s which focused on familiar rather than unfamiliar faces. This approach led to the development of a number of 'modular' models of face recognition. These models assumed that different aspects of face recognition were processed by separate units or modules. Before examining some of these models in detail it is important to explore some of the studies which shaped their basic concepts.

Studies of face recognition

Prosopagnosia

Prosopagnosia is a disorder which is caused by cerebral injury and results in the inability to recognise faces. Prosopagnosic patients are often unable to recognise friends, family or the faces of famous people. Some are even unable to recognise themselves in a mirror. However, prosopagnosia does not affect the ability to recognise all other objects. Bruyer *et al.* (1983) have described the case of a farmer who could not recognise the faces of his family but could recognise his cows.

Prosopagnosia is not a result of forgetting people since prosopagnosic patients are able to recognise people using a variety of cues, such as their voice or clothing.

Since prosopagnosia is a result of damage to the cortex it tends to affect each patient slightly differently. For example, Bruyer *et al.* (1983) studied a patient who could recognise that photographs taken from different angles were of the same person and could recognise expressions. However, he could not recognise familiar faces. In contrast, Malone *et al.* (1982) described a patient who could recognise familiar faces but could not match different photographs of unfamiliar ones. These cases suggest that there is a difference in recognition of familiar and unfamiliar faces.

Is face recognition a special process?

The studies of prosopagnosic patients seem to indicate that face recognition is a separate or special process. However, Ellis and Young (1989) point out that many prosopagnosic patients have problems in identifying some other objects as well as faces. Also, it may be that the damage which causes prosopagnosia renders the patient incapable of making the slight distinctions needed to recognise faces. Despite these doubts there does seem to be some evidence that there are specific mechanisms for recognising faces. For example, DeRenzi (1986) described a patient who could not recognise friends and relatives by their faces. However, he was able to make fine distinctions about other objects. For example, he could identify his handwriting from that of others and could pick out a Siamese cat from pictures of cats. This seems to suggest that he suffered from damage to the mechanisms for recognising faces only. Further evidence for face-specific processing is provided by neurophysiological studies which have shown that there are neurones that respond to particular aspects of faces. Perrett *et al.* (1986) have found five types of cells in the temporal lobe of macaques that respond to different facial views (full face, profile, etc.).

Ellis and Young (1989) examined the question 'Are faces special?' and concluded that the process of face recognition is *special* but not *unique*. Since faces play such an important role in our lives the mechanisms for recognising faces have special significance but do not seem to be entirely different from the mechanisms for other types of recognition.

Affective and communicative information

Faces are important in our lives, not just because they are our primary means of identification, but because they convey social information. Faces are used to express emotions (affective information) and to convey important signals (communicative information).

In an analysis of face recognition, Bruce (1988) claims that these social aspects of faces can be regarded as separate from the identification and recognition of faces. She quotes evidence about prosopagnosic patients who can recognise expressions but cannot identify faces, and others who can identify faces but have difficulty in recognising expressions. Similarly there are cases of prosopagnosic patients who cannot recognise faces but can identify phonemes when they are mouthed (in effect 'lip-read'), and other patients with alexia ('word blindness') who can recognise faces but find it difficult to judge phonemes.

Face recognition – features or configuration?

There are two main types of information that we might use to recognise faces. First, we could use information provided by the individual features, such as the shape of the mouth, nose, etc. Each person has their own set of features and once they have been identified we can recognise them. The second type of information is provided by the configuration of the features. The overall arrangement of the features could be as important as the features themselves.

There is evidence that features are significant in face recognition. However, some features are more important than others. Studies suggest that hair, face outline and eyes are more important than lower internal features, particularly the nose (Shepherd, Davies and Ellis, 1981). Different features seem to be important for familiar and unfamiliar faces. Ellis, Shepherd and Davies (1979) found that recognition of familiar faces was better using internal rather than external features. However, recognition of unfamiliar faces was equally successful using internal or external features.

There is also a considerable body of evidence that suggests that the configuration of features is important. Haig (1984) used computer displays of faces that could be adjusted and found that slight changes in the arrangement of features impaired recognition. Further evidence that configuration is important was shown by Young *et al*. (1987). They showed participants photographs that combined the bottom half of one famous face and the top half of another. Participants were asked to name the top half. This was much more difficult when the two halves were closely aligned than when they were not aligned. They argue that this is because close alignment creates a new configuration.

Bruce (1988) suggests that information about both features and the configuration of features seems to be important in recognising faces. She suggests that the overall configuration may be used to guide the analysis of the detail of the features. Homa *et al*. (1976) have reported a 'face superiority effect' which provides evidence for this view. They asked participants to identify a feature that they had just been shown. For example, after seeing a face they might be shown a set of noses and asked which was the one they had seen. Participants were more accurate when the feature was presented in a normal face configuration than when the face was scrambled. This suggests that perception of face configuration precedes the perception of the details of the features.

Methodological considerations

Many of the experiments described above and throughout the rest of this chapter have studied the recognition of pictures. This approach has advantages since pictures can be a standard stimulus that can be presented in a standard way (time, distance, etc.). The use of pictures therefore offers great control over the study. However, there are concerns about this approach (e.g. Bruce, 1988). Primarily the recognition of *pictures of faces* may not be the same as the recognition of *real faces* (in other words, the studies lack ecological validity). Real faces differ from pictures in two main ways. First, real faces are three-dimensional (3-D) whereas pictures are two-dimensional (2-D). A 3-D view offers more information than a 2-D view and therefore might reveal aspects of faces that a 2-D view cannot. Secondly, real faces are animate but pictures are not. Real faces constantly move, change expression and convey information about speech. Pictures do not provide this type of information.

Write brief answers to the following questions:

1. What is the main symptom of prosopagnosia?
2. What evidence is there to suggest that familiar and unfamiliar faces are processed differently?

Bruce and Young's model

The influential model of face recognition proposed by Bruce and Young (1986) was in part an extension of earlier models such as that of Hay and Young (1982). The model was an attempt to account for the diverse research findings about face recognition. Bruce and Young argued that evidence suggests there are different types of information that can be obtained from faces. For example, a face can provide us with information about a person's identity but it can also provide us with information about a person's mood. Bruce and Young argue that the different types of information are processed independently, and have proposed eight components to their model (see Figure 6.1).

In the model all processing starts with *structural encoding* which can provide visual descriptions at different levels. View-centred descriptions are used to analyse information about facial expression and speech whereas expression-independent descriptions provide more abstract information about the identity of the face. One of the key features of the model is that familiar and unfamiliar faces are processed differently.

Familiar faces are analysed using expression-independent description which can then be compared to descriptions in the *face recognition units* (FRUs). These are our store of faces we know and these can be compared to the expression-independent description by our cognitive system. This process can be aided by information from the *person identity nodes* (PINs). The person identity nodes store information about people, such as their job, friends, interests, etc. It is at this level that person, rather than face, recognition occurs. For example, you may see a person and recognise their face. Moments later you may 'place' that person as someone who works in the local bank. Once identity has been established, the last component in the processing of familiar

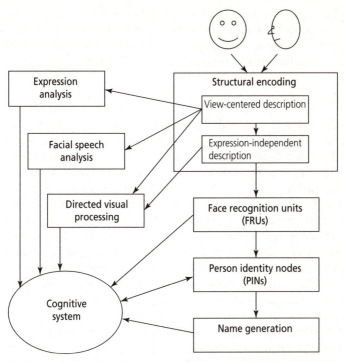

Figure 6.1 **Bruce and Young's model of face recognition (based on Bruce and Young, 1986). Reproduced with permission from *The British Journal of Psychology*, © The British Psychological Society**

faces is *name generation*. The model assumes that names can only be accessed via person identity nodes.

Unfamiliar faces are analysed using view-centred descriptions (they cannot be analysed with expression-independent descriptions since the face is not known). This analysis can be used for *expression analysis* to provide information about the person's emotional state, and for *facial speech analysis* to aid speech perception. In some circumstances some information about faces has to be processed selectively. If we want to remember a face or make a decision about a face we may have to attend carefully to certain aspects. In these circumstances the model suggests that *directed visual processing* is used. All of these components can be used with unfamiliar and familiar faces. However, unfamiliar faces can *only* be processed with these components.

The final component of the model is the *cognitive system*. This is the component that makes decisions, initiates responses and performs functions that are not performed in the rest of the model. Bruce (1988) likens it to the 'central executive' in the working memory.

Evaluation

This model seems to provide a good explanation of the research findings discussed earlier in the chapter. One of the central assumptions of the model is that familiar and unfamiliar faces are analysed differently. This is supported by evidence from both cognitive neuropsychology and cognitive psychology. Malone *et al*. (1982) described one prosopagnosic patient who could match photographs of unfamiliar faces but could not recognise famous faces. They described another patient who could recognise famous faces but could not match different photographs of an unfamiliar face. Ellis *et al*. (1979) found that participants relied on different features when identifying familiar or unfamiliar faces. The model also suggests that there are separate components for face recognition, expression analysis and facial speech analysis. Bruce (1988) has described evidence from a number of prosopagnosic patients that suggests that affective and speech information is processed separately from face recognition.

Another important feature of the model is the assumption that names can only be accessed via the person identity nodes. This assumption is supported by most studies of brain-damaged patients. These often show that, when presented with familiar faces, patients can remember information about the person but not their names. For example, Flude, Ellis and Kay (1989) described a patient who, when presented with familiar faces, could recall the occupations of 85 per cent of people but could only recall 15 per cent of their names. There is also psychological evidence for this assumption. Young, Hay and Ellis (1985) asked participants to keep a diary record of the problems they had in recognising faces (see Key research study 4 on p. 112). A common experience was to recognise a face and recall information about the person (occupation, friends, etc.) but to be unable to remember the name. There was not one incident of recalling a name without recalling information about the person. The model also predicts that sometimes face recognition units may be activated but there is a failure to retrieve information from the person identity nodes. This suggests that we sometimes are able to recognise a face but cannot 'place it', that is, we cannot recall any information about the face. This is a common experience and was found on 233 occasions in the Young *et al.* (1985) diary study.

Although the Bruce and Young model was influential, it does not explain all aspects of face recognition. Bruce (1988) herself claimed that one of the fundamental problems of the model is that it does not explain how a face recognition unit is formed. The model assumes that familiar faces are recognised by face recognition units but it does not explain how or when an unfamiliar face becomes familiar enough to have a face recognition unit. Another assumption of the model is that names can only be accessed via person identity nodes. However, de Hann, Young and Newcombe (1991) have described the case of an amnesiac patient who was able to name famous people from pictures of their faces but was unable to recall any information about the person. She seemed to have damage to her person identity nodes but yet was able to generate names. A final problem of the model is that some components are not clearly defined. This is particularly true of the cognitive system which Bruce (1988) admits is a 'catch-all' component. Thus, if something is not performed elsewhere in the model, it is assumed that the cognitive system does it. It is also not clear whether semantic information is stored in the person identity nodes or is accessed via them.

List the eight components of the Bruce and Young model. Explain the function of each component.

Progress exercise

Burton, Bruce and Johnson's interactive activation model

Burton, Bruce and Johnson (1990) and Burton and Bruce (1992) have proposed an alternative model of face recognition (Figure 6.2). This model uses many of the original concepts of the Bruce and Young

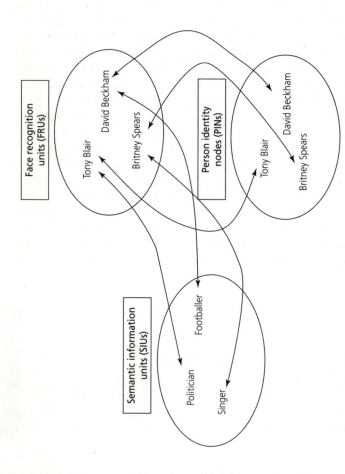

Figure 6.2 Burton, Bruce and Johnson's model of face recognition (based on Burton, Bruce and Johnson, 1990). Reproduced with permission from *The British Journal of Psychology*, © The British Psychological Society

model, but, as Young and Bruce (1991) point out, it has been 'recast in terms of an interactive activation model' (see below). One major difference is that in this model there are three distinct pools of information instead of the eight separate components in the Bruce and Young model.

The three pools of information are:

1. **Face recognition units (FRUs)**. These are units that are activated whenever a familiar face is presented. They are view-independent (that is, they can be activated by the face from different angles, wearing different expressions, etc.). They are activated maximally by specific patterns of features.
2. **Person identity nodes (PINs)**. It is at this level that decisions about familiarity are taken. The PINs can be activated both by FRUs and by names and voices.
3. **Semantic information units (SIUs)**. These contain information about a person, such as their interests, occupation, etc.

The three pools of information are linked by bi-directional excitatory links. This means that recognition in any pool can trigger information from another. Thus, identification of a person can trigger semantic information about them, but semantic knowledge about a person might equally trigger identification. Faces are recognised as familiar when they trigger the appropriate PIN. The PIN could also be triggered by voice, name or other information. In this model, decisions about familiarity are made at PINs not FRUs. Both the PIN and the FRU act as nodes but do not themselves contain information about visual or semantic features. Burton *et al*. suggest that it is the person rather than the face that is recognised. Another feature of the model is that, although there is excitation between the pools of information, there is inhibition within the pools. Thus activation of one PIN will inhibit the activation of another.

In the original model by Burton *et al*. it was suggested that there was a separate pool for name input to the PINs. However, in a revised version of the model, suggested by Burton and Bruce (1992), names are mixed in with other semantic information in the SIUs. They argue that the evidence does not support the existence of separate name units and that the reason that names are difficult to access is that they are individual, whereas many people share other information. For example,

I am only aware of one person called 'Tony Blair' but I am aware of many politicians, I know of a number of people who have been Prime Minister of Britain, etc.

Evaluation

There are a number of advantages of the Burton *et al.* approach over the Bruce and Young model. First, Eysenck and Keane (1995) claim that it is more precise and provides a more detailed interactive activation model compared to the Bruce and Young model. Secondly, this model seems to account for the findings of de Hann *et al.* (1991). They described a patient who could match names to faces of famous people but could not recall any autobiographical information. This model suggests that face and name information can be linked without access to autobiographical information. Finally, there is a variety of evidence to support the interactive activation model. For example, Ellis, Burton, Young and Flude (1997) have studied the effect of repetition priming between parts of famous faces and the whole faces. As predicted by the interactive activation model, recognition of part of a face was primed more by the recognition of the whole face than by recognition of the same part.

Despite the advantages of this model there are still a number of problems. As with the Bruce and Young theory, this model does not explain the development of face recognition units. When do unfamiliar faces become familiar enough to have a face recognition unit, and how is the view-independent unit formed? The model concentrates on the recognition of familiar rather than unfamiliar faces. A further problem (acknowledged by Burton *et al.*) is that the model does not fully specify what information about faces is fed to the FRUs.

Young and Bruce (1991) point out that face recognition is a complex process involving many interacting factors. They suggest that current models should be regarded as a stage in the understanding of this complex process.

Farah – holistic analysis of faces

Farah and her colleagues (1990, 1994, 1998) have proposed an alternative view of face recognition to that of Burton and Bruce. Farah (1990) originally developed her theory after analysing the selective problems caused by different types of visual agnosia. She compared the disruption caused by prosopagnosia, object agnosia and alexia. Patients with prosopagnosia have difficulty in recognising faces but often can recognise other objects and words. Patients with object agnosia have difficulty in recognising objects but not necessarily faces. Patients with alexia have difficulty in recognising written words but understand spoken language and usually have good object and face recognition. Farah suggested that this indicates that there are two underlying representational abilities that result in two forms of analysis:

1. Holistic analysis, in which the overall structure of the object is processed. Farah describes objects that are analysed holistically as those that 'undergo little or no decomposition'. These objects are recognised as a whole not by their parts.
2. Analysis of parts, in which the parts of an object and the relationship between the parts are processed. Some objects can be 'decomposed' into few parts and others into many parts.

Most objects require holistic and part analysis but Farah argues that the cognitive neuropsychological evidence suggests that face recognition relies on **holistic analysis**. However, a task such as reading demands analysis of the parts since understanding a sentence requires recognition of the letters that constitute each word and then recognition of the words that make the sentence. In prosopagnosia it is the holistic analysis that is affected and objects that rely on analysis of parts, such as reading, are unimpaired. The reverse is true of alexia as here it is the analysis of the parts that is disrupted but the ability to recognise faces by holistic analysis is unaffected.

Farah *et al.* (1998) claim that face recognition is special because faces "constitute an extreme case of stimuli that rely on holistic shape representation". However, they argue that face recognition is not necessarily discontinuous from recognition of other objects since many will require some holistic analysis. Farah (2000) has also claimed that studies of prosopagnosic patients provide evidence that there is a 'face module' in the brain. This is supported by magnetic resonance imaging (MRI) studies which have revealed a region of the brain, the lateral fusiform gyrus, which is specialised for dealing with face recognition (Ishai *et al.*, 1999)

Evaluation

There are a number of sources of evidence for the view that faces are recognised holistically. In her analysis of visual agnosia Farah (1990) found that there is a double dissociation between prosopagnosia and alexia. That is, there are many cases of prosopagnosia without alexia and there are many cases of alexia without prosopagnosia. However, both conditions frequently occur with object agnosia. This seems to be evidence that the brain mechanisms and processes for face recognition are different from those for word recognition. Farah (1994) has tested the idea that face recognition depends on holistic analysis to a greater degree than other objects. Participants were shown drawings of faces and houses and were asked to name each drawing (faces and houses). They were then shown either whole pictures of houses and faces or pictures of a single feature of a face or house. They were asked to identify whether a named feature (e.g. nose or door) was part of a picture they had previously named. The accuracy of recognising house features was much the same whether a whole house or a single feature was presented. However, recognition of facial features was much better in the whole face condition than the single feature condition. This seems to indicate that faces are recognised holistically but other objects, such as houses, are recognised more by analysis of parts. In another experiment Farah *et al*. (1998) investigated whether faces are perceived holistically. They showed participants a face followed by a mask (which was either a whole face or scrambled face parts) and then another face. The participants were asked to decide whether the two faces were the same. Farah *et al*. argued that if faces are analysed holistically then the whole mask should cause more interference in the recognition task than the mask consisting of face parts. This is precisely what they found with faces but when a similar test was done with words, whole and part words caused similar disruption to recognition. They suggest that this is evidence of two representational abilities: holistic, which is essential for faces but not used for words, and part-based, which is essential for words but not used for faces.

Farah *et al*. (1998) also point to converging evidence from cognitive neuroscience and cognitive science which supports the theory of holistic face representation. The theory predicts that neurones responding to faces (or face cells) should function as templates. These cells should respond differently to different faces and presentation of a scrambled face should abolish the response. Farah *et al*. (1998) cite evidence that this is the case (e.g. Desimone, 1991). They also note that recent computer models of face recognition have favoured holistic representation rather than the traditional approach of using facial features or analysis of parts (e.g. Turk and Pentland, 1991).

One of the main problems of this theory is that it concentrates on the perceptual aspects of face recognition. However there is much more to face recognition than simply perceiving a face. We use faces to decide whether a person is familiar or not and as a means of identifying people. Faces convey a lot of information and are linked to our knowledge about the person. In their model Burton, Bruce and Johnson (1990) describe three pools of information: face recognition units, person identity nodes and semantic information units. The Farah approach concentrates on the first of these only. This may be related to another problem identified by Eysenck and Keane (2000) which is that Farah focuses on *apperceptive* rather than *associative* agnosia (that is agnosia which is linked to impaired perception rather than agnosia that is linked with an impaired ability to associate meaning with an object).

Face recognition in 'real life'

The ability to recognise faces plays a central part in much of our lives. Our social interaction with friends, family and colleagues relies on our ability to recognise and identify faces. The ability to recognise faces becomes crucial when we witness a crime. Police rely on witnesses to build a picture of the suspect, to try to select the person from a book of 'mug-shots' and to identify the person from a line-up. The topic of eyewitness testimony is discussed in detail in another book in this series (*Memory and Forgetting*, Henderson, 1999). However, there are several issues relating to face recognition that are worth mentioning here.

Bruce (1988) has highlighted an apparent paradox in the accuracy of face recognition. Laboratory studies of face recognition tend to show that face recognition is very accurate (for example, Brown *et al*. (1977) found that, even after a delay of two days, participants could recognise 96 per cent of faces). However, there are many examples of false identification of suspects and these suggest that face recognition by witnesses is not accurate (see, for example, the Devlin report, 1976).

One reason for the discrepancy may be the artificial nature of laboratory studies. In a typical laboratory experiment participants are shown pictures or photographs of people and then some time later they are asked to identify the *same* picture or photograph. A witness will often see a suspect from one particular viewpoint. They may just glimpse the person and have a mental image of the face. However, they are unlikely to see the person in exactly the same way or from the same point of view again. The pictures they see of the person, or the perspective in a line-up, will be *different*. A number of studies have shown that, if there is some form of transformation (or change) between the original stimulus and the stimulus participants are asked to identify, the accuracy of identification is reduced (e.g. Davies *et al.*, 1978).

Another aspect of face recognition that is important in police investigations is the use of Photofit kits. The assumption is that witnesses can picture the constituent parts of a face and use photographs of eyes, mouths, noses, etc. to compose an accurate likeness of the suspect. However, some studies suggest that the likeness of suspects produced by this procedure is generally poor (Ellis *et al.*, 1978). One reason for this is that faces are identified by configuration as much as features and, if Farah (1990) is correct, faces are perceived and recognised holistically. Searching for individual features away from the overall configuration may produce inaccuracies. Haig (1984) has shown that small changes to the positioning of features such as eyes and mouth can produce the impression of a completely different face. Developments in computing and graphic software have led to the development of the E-fit. This allows for global manipulation of images, blending between features and subtle variations in the configuration of the features, and seems to produce much more realistic images of people than the Photofit (Bruce and Young, 1998).

Summary

Faces are important and complex objects. The processes involved in the recognition of faces have been studied extensively in the last few decades. Physiological evidence suggests that faces are processed separately from other patterns. For example, there are cells in the visual cortex which respond to faces only. Prosopagnosia is a disorder that affects face recognition but leaves most other visual and memory functions intact. Psychological evidence suggests that there is a difference in the recognition of familiar and unfamiliar faces and that information about speech and emotions is processed independently from face recognition. Evidence also suggests that information about both features and configuration is used in face analysis. Bruce and Young (1986) proposed a model of face recognition that was comprised of eight components. It assumed that unfamiliar faces were processed by analysing expression, facial speech and specific facial features. Familiar faces were processed by using face recognition units which led to information about identity which, in turn, led to information about names. This was an influential model which explained many of the findings about face recognition. However, some aspects of the model are not fully explained, such as the formation of face recognition units and the function of the cognitive system. Furthermore, the model cannot explain why information about names can be retrieved without some autobiographical information. Burton, Bruce and Johnson (1990) have put forward an alternative interactive activation model which proposes that there are three pools of information which have bi-directional links. This model is able to explain how information about names can be retrieved without first accessing autobiographical information. However, it does not fully explain how face recognition units are formed. Farah and her colleagues have proposed that, unlike many other objects, faces are perceived and recognised holistically. The theory was originally based on an analysis of different types of visual agnosia but has also gained support from studies in cognition, neuroscience and cognitive science. This approach tends to concentrate on the perceptual rather than semantic aspects of face recognition.

Compare the Bruce and Young model with the Burton, Bruce and Johnson model.

What features did Burton, Bruce and Johnson retain from the Bruce and Young model?

Outline the major differences between the two models.

How do these models differ from the approach taken by Farah?

Review exercise

Further reading

Eysenck, M.W. and Keane, M.T. (2000) *Cognitive Psychology – A Student's Handbook* (4th edn). Hove, UK: Psychology Press. This is one of the few cognitive psychology textbooks that has a good section on face recognition.

Young, A. and Bruce, V. (1998). *Face and Mind*. Oxford: Oxford University Press. This is an advanced textbook written by two of the foremost researchers in this area. It has too much detail for A level work but is excellent for anyone with a particular interest in the topic.

7

Study aids

IMPROVING YOUR ESSAY-WRITING SKILLS

At this point in the book you have acquired the knowledge necessary to tackle the exam itself. Answering exam questions is a skill, and this chapter shows you how to improve this skill. Examiners obviously have first-hand knowledge about what goes wrong in exams. For example, candidates frequently do not answer the question that has been set – rather they answer the one that they hoped would come up – or they do not make effective use of the knowledge they have, but just 'dump their psychology' on the page and hope the examiner will sort it out for them. A grade C answer usually contains appropriate material but tends to be limited in detail and commentary. To lift such an answer to a grade A or B may require no more than a little more detail, better use of material and coherent organisation. It is important to appreciate that it may not involve writing at any greater length, but might even necessitate the elimination of passages that do not add to the quality of the answer, and some elaboration of those that do.

By studying the essays presented in this chapter and the examiner's comments, you can learn how to turn your grade C answer into a grade A. Typically it only involves an extra 4 marks out of 24. Please note that marks given by the examiner in the practice essays should be used as a guide only and are not definitive. They represent the 'raw' marks that would be likely to be given to answers to AQA(A) questions. In the AQA(A) examination, an examiner would award a maximum of

12 marks for knowledge and understanding (called Assessment Objective 1 – AO1) and 12 marks for evaluation, analysis and commentary (Assessment Objective 2 – AO2). The details of this marking scheme are given in Appendix C of Paul Humphreys' title in this series, *Exam Success in AEB Psychology* and the forthcoming title, *Exam Success in AQA(A) Psychology*. Remember that these are the raw marks and not the same as those given on the examination certificate received ultimately by the candidate, because all examining boards are required to use a common standardised system – the Uniform Mark Scale (UMS) – which adjusts all raw scores to a single standard across all boards.

The essays given here are notionally written by an 18-year-old in thirty minutes, and are marked bearing that in mind. It is important when writing to such a tight time limit that you make every sentence count. Each essay in this chapter is followed by detailed comments about its strengths and weaknesses. The most common problems to watch out for are:

- Failure to answer the question but reproducing a model answer to a similar question which you have pre-learned.
- Not delivering the right balance between description and evaluation/ analysis. Remember they are always weighted 50/50.
- Writing 'everything you know' about a topic in the hope that something will get credit and the examiner will sort your work out for you. Remember that excellence demands selectivity, so improvements can often be made by removing material that is irrelevant to the question set and elaborating material that *is* relevant.
- Failing to use your material effectively. It is not enough to place the information on the page; you must also show the examiner that you are using it to make a particular point.

For more ideas on how to write good essays you should consult *Exam Success in AEB Psychology* and the forthcoming title *Exam Success in AQA(A) Psychology* (both by Paul Humphreys) in this series.

Practice essay 1

Discuss, with reference to both theories *and* studies, the nature of selective attention. (24 marks)

AQA (AEB) 1996 Summer

Psychologists find it extremely difficult to define what attention actually is. One description is 'the focusing of our attention'. We also talk about attention as concentration. There are several types of attention, one of which is focused (or selective) attention. This is the ability to pick out one stimulus from a variety of others. A way of studying this is by examining auditory attention.

Early research into auditory attention was done by Cherry (1953) who investigated the 'cocktail party phenomenon'. This suggests we have the ability to be deep in conversation, then someone else in the room starts to talk about you and you then eventually notice this by switching your attention. Cherry used the dichotic listening experiment and shadowing. This is when two messages are played at the exact same time. Cherry found that the participants were able to repeat one of the messages, but when asked about the other, they had no knowledge of what the message contained, only what the physical aspects of the message were. This tends to suggest that the ears work as two separate channels, which enables us to block information out.

Broadbent also used an experiment to study auditory attention by the use of the split-span procedure. He found that his participants found the ear-to-ear a lot easier than the pair-by-pair condition, as they could switch from channel to channel. From this information, Broadbent developed the 'Filter model' (1958). This suggests we have a limited capacity, which means, although we hear and only briefly store infor-mation, it must be filtered so that only one piece of information is left, in order to respond. This proposes that the filter blocks out the rest of the information and that we have the ability to change the bias of the filter to let in the desired information.

This model in one way backs up what Cherry said about some information being let through and some being stopped. But it does not fully explain the 'cocktail phenomenon'. Soon after Broadbent's model was produced, several psychologists carried out experiments which disproved his theory. One of which was Moray (1959), who found that a third of the time most people noticed their names in unshadowed conversations, which suggests the information is not fully blocked out. Gray and Wedderburn (1960) also disproved Broadbent's model.

Treisman created 'the Attenuator model' to attempt to explain auditory attention. This model proposes that all information we hear is filtered, but it is passed through at different volumes. It suggests that some information is attenuated. Some words are easily detected because they are important and can be detected even if they are attenuated. This model is much better at explaining the 'cocktail party phenomenon' and also the experiments carried out by Moray, Gray and Wedderburn. Treisman also found that we hear information we expect to hear and that we don't hear information we do not expect to hear. The problems with the 'Attenuator model' and the 'Filter model' are how does the filter know what information to let through and what information not to let through. These two models are 'Early Selection Models' which means that information is selected early in processing before the content is analysed.

The 'Pertinence Model' produced by Deutsch and Deutsch entails late selection rather than early selection. This model states that all information goes to the senses and it is then sent for further attention all at the same volume (unlike the Attenuator model). It is then selected for its pertinence, which is how relevant it is, then, depending on your predisposition, some information is let through.

Evidence for this model was presented by Mackay, whose experiment showed that even if some information is not noticed it has an influence so it must have been processed to some extent. Treisman and Greffen carried out an experiment, which disproved the Pertinence model as the words from both messages were not heard equally in each ear. So it tended to support the Attenuator model.

These three theories have only looked at single filter models. The only difference between them seems to be where the filter is in the model and what it does to the information. Auditory Attention seems to be too complicated to be explained by these three simple models. These models also lacked an explanation of practice, difficulty was ignored and they were also too simple.

Examiner's comment

This essay addresses the question well and mentions experiments and theories that potentially could gain a very good mark. However, much of the discussion of experiments and theories is limited in both description and evaluation. This tends to limit the essay to a grade C answer, with a mark of 13 out of 24 (6 for skill A and 7 for skill B). The overall structure and scope of the essay are good but it lacks detail throughout.

The initial description of experiments by Cherry and Broadbent is reasonable but it does not describe their methods and findings in an entirely clear way. It is therefore difficult to understand the conclusions drawn from the studies. For example, the candidate mentions the split-span experiments but does not describe what they are. Thus the conclusion that participants can switch from channel to channel does not make sense. The description of Broadbent's filter model is succinct but accurate. The candidate has also attempted to evaluate the model by analysing the experimental evidence for and against the model, but again lacks detail. Why is this model supported by Cherry's findings and how did Gray and Wedderburn 'disprove' Broadbent's ideas?

The description of Treisman's model is again accurate but again it could be more detailed. The use of examples would help to illustrate the ideas of the model. The candidate refers to some good studies to evaluate Treisman's model but again these lack detail. Why is this model a better explanation of the cocktail party phenomenon? Details of the Gray and Wedderburn study would have provided very good support for the model. The theoretical problem of early selection models is described well. The Deutsch and Deutsch model is also discussed accurately but lacks elaboration. There are no details of the MacKay experiment or of Treisman and Geffen's study of early versus late selection.

Finally, the conclusion shows that the candidate has a good understanding of this topic generally, but the points raised could be illustrated better. For example, the study by Allport *et al.* (1972) questions the validity of the single channel models.

Practice essay 2

Describe and evaluate two theories which seek to explain divided attention. (24 marks)

Candidate's answer

Divided attention concerns the ability to perform two or more tasks simultaneously. There are three factors, which affect the performance of dual tasks: (i) Task difficulty (ii) Task practice (iii) Task similarity. Many different theories have been suggested and I will cover two in this essay.

The first one is Kahneman's (1973) 'Limited central capacity theory'. Kahneman sees attention as a skill rather than a process and argues that there is just one central processor, which allocates a central pool of attentional resources in a flexible manner across a variety of different tasks. The central processor has a limited capacity, which it can allocate at any one time. Tasks requiring little capacity need little mental effort and therefore leave more room for performing additional tasks, and so if a task requires a large amount of mental effort it will leave no room for other tasks. The amount of mental effort depends on the difficulty of the task and whether it has been practised before. The amount of capacity (mental effort) available depends on arousal, e.g. alertness or how awake we are.

This model is more flexible than previous models as it takes into account arousal, practice and difficulty. For example, it seems to explain results of experiments like that of Spelke who found that two difficult tasks could be done simultaneously when they were practised. This theory, however, does not explain how much capacity there is. It is quite a 'general' model of attention, it describes attention as one thing. It doesn't explain why it is more difficult to do two similar tasks at once than two dissimilar tasks (e.g. it is difficult to listen to two conversations through headphones but you can listen to one conversation and watch a screen).

Another theory is Allport's module resource theory. Allport suggests that attention consists of several specialised information-processing modules for information, each with its own resources and capacity, rather than one central processor. Tasks that are similar use the same module resources and interfere with one another if done at the same time, thus preventing dual task performances. Tasks that are different can be done at the same time without interfering with each other. This theory accounts for the way that dual tasks can be done and attention divided if the tasks are non-similar. It therefore explains how piano players can read music and shadow spoken messages.

This theory does not, however, account for how many modules there are, or what types of modules exist, e.g. students were trained to do two tasks that should have demanded similar modules. However, speech production systems are separate, perhaps accounting for the ability of some translators to listen, translate and speak their language simultaneously. It also doesn't explain how the modules interact so smoothly with each other.

The different theories seem to explain different aspects of dual attention experiments. Kahneman explains the influence of practice better but Allport explains similarity better. You would have to look at a number of different theories, not just two, to get an overall picture of how divided attention works.

Examiner's comment

This is a good essay that answers the question well and has a reasonable-to-good level of description and evaluation. The essay is likely to score 14 out of 24 (7 for skill A and 7 for skill B). Although the essay seems short it discusses a lot of ideas in a succinct manner.

Kahneman's model is generally described well, although there is no description of one of the key features of the model, the allocation of attention. The evaluation of the model is good on ideas but often assumes the examiner knows what the candidate means since it does not explain the ideas carefully. For example, the candidate points out that the Kahneman model 'sees attention as one thing'. This may be a very valid point but it needs to be explained carefully. If the candidate had stated that 'the model assumes that attention is controlled by one central processor' it would make the point clear and would show good skill B. The evaluation of the model lacks elaboration generally and would be improved with more detail.

The description of Allport's model is clear and accurate but would have been improved with a few more examples. The evaluation of the model uses some very good ideas but is not clear. More detail about the problems of the model would have cleared up any ambiguity in the essay and would add elaboration which is an important part of skill B.

KEY RESEARCH SUMMARIES

Article 1

Allport, D.A., Antonis, B. and Reynolds, P. (1972). On the division of attention: a disproof of the single channel hypothesis. *Quarterly Journal of Experimental Psychology*, 24, 225–35.

Aim

When this study was published all the contemporary models of selective attention assumed that attention was controlled by a single processor (operating through a single channel).The aim of the study was to examine this assumption. The study used two different experimental methods.

Method 1

In the first experiment participants were asked to perform a dual task. All participants were asked to shadow a female voice reading extracts from Orwell's 'Selected Essays' presented to the right ear via headphones. All the participants were also asked to learn a list at the same time. They were allocated to one of three conditions. For Group 1 a list of 15 words was presented at a rate of 1 every 3 seconds to the left ear of the headphones in a male voice. Group 2 were presented with exactly the same words at exactly the same rate but the words were presented visually on a screen. Group 3 were presented with 15 pictures on a screen at the rate of 1 every 3 seconds. The pictures were representations of the 15 words used in conditions 1 and 2.

Results 1

Although the task of learning 15 words appears to be similar in each condition, Allport and his colleagues found that the mode of presentation greatly influenced the percentage recalled. Group 1 only recalled an average of 55 per cent of the list, whereas group 2 recalled 68 per cent. However, group 3 showed by far the best recall with an average rate of 92 per cent.

A control study revealed that the percentage recalled in the three conditions when there was no concurrent shadowing task was about the same (about 95 per cent). This shows that the mode of presentation of the list did not itself affect recall.

Method 2

Experienced musicians (third-year undergraduates studying music) were asked to shadow continuous prose whilst simultaneously playing music from a score. The score was previously unseen and the participants' performance was recorded so that it could be graded. The participants were instructed to do both tasks to the best of their ability and told that neither task was more important than the other. Both the shadowing and the piano playing had an easy and a difficult condition. The easy shadowing task used extracts of humorous prose but the difficult condition used extracts from early Norse history that included many low-frequency words. The piano playing was either exam grade II (easy) or grade IV (difficult). Participants were studied in two sessions.

Results 2

During session 1 the participants made very few errors when the easy conditions were used but did make more errors when the difficult conditions were used. However, by session 2 the participants made very few errors using either the easy or difficult conditions. Their performance on each of the concurrent tasks, shadowing and piano playing, was not significantly worse than performing either alone.

Discussion

The results from these two experiments seem difficult to reconcile with the notion of a single all-purpose processor. Research before this study had tended to concentrate on dichotic listening tasks and had suggested that there is a limit to attentional capacity. The fact that participants could perform the complex tasks of shadowing, sight-reading and piano playing simultaneously with little loss in efficiency suggests the limit is flexible. However, it is the results from the first experiment that challenge the idea of a single processor. Allport *et al*. showed that learning a list of words via headphones or on a screen or as pictures produced roughly the same degree of recall. Yet when this task is combined with the concurrent task of shadowing speech the mode of presentation produces great differences in performance. Participants found it easy to learn a list of pictures on a screen and to shadow speech. They found the task of learning a list of words presented to one ear and shadowing speech in the other ear very difficult. These differences between the conditions cannot be explained by task difficulty. The explanation seems to be that there are different resources for different tasks. Watching pictures on a screen requires different resources from listening and repeating speech. However, listening to a list of words and listening to speech require the same resources. This experiment suggests that attention is controlled by a number of independent processors operating in parallel.

Article 2

Schneider, W. and Shiffrin, R.M. (1977). Controlled and automatic human information processing: detection, search and attention. *Psychological Review*, **84, 1–66.**

Aim

There seems to be a difference in the attentional processes for novel/difficult tasks and well-practised/easy tasks. The two types of processing have been labelled controlled and automatic. The aim of this study was to investigate the development of automaticity. Since Schneider and Shiffrin embarked on a large program of research to investigate automaticity only a selection of their results can be reported here (see also the companion paper by Shiffrin and Schneider, 1977).

Method

Schneider and Shiffrin used a visual search task to study the develop-ment of automaticity. Participants were asked to search for a target item (or items) amongst a number of displays. The target item/s were letters or numbers and these were shown to the participants before each series of displays. The participants were asked to memorise the characters (these target items were called the 'memory set'). Once the targets had been memorised participants were shown a fixation dot followed by a series of displays containing various characters. The displays were called 'frames'. The participants' task was to decide whether a target item appeared in any of the frames.

A number of variables were manipulated during the research program. One was the memory-set size or the number of target items to be memorised. A second was the frame size, that is, the number of items in each display. A third variable was the frame time, which is how long each display was presented. The crucial variable was the *mapping* of targets and display characters. In the *consistent mapping condition* the target items were taken from one set of characters (e.g. letters) and the distracter items in the display were taken from another (e.g. numbers). In the *varied mapping condition* the target items and the distracter items were mixed (e.g. both could be letters and numbers).

The dependent variables in the series of experiments were the speed of the decision of whether a target item was present or not and the accuracy of the decision.

There were several key results of this study. First, Schneider and Shiffrin compared how long the frames had to be presented before the participants reached a minimum level of accuracy of response (set at 95 per cent). They found a large difference between the two mapping conditions. The frames only had to be presented for an average of 70 ms in the consistent mapping condition, but in the varied mapping condition the frames had to be presented for an average of 210 ms to obtain the same degree of accuracy. The second main finding was that the memory-set size and the frame size had a great effect in the varied mapping condition. As either of these variables increased so did the time taken to achieve accurate decisions. This was still the case even after extended practice. However, after practice, neither of these variables affected the performance in the consistent mapping condition to any great degree. The times taken to achieve accurate decisions were nearly the same when the memory set was 1, 2 or 4 items. Similarly the times for a frame size of 1, 2 or 4 items remained nearly constant.

The results seem to demonstrate a number of important points about the development of automatic processing. The first part of the experiment showed that memory-set size affected both the consistent mapping condition and the varied mapping condition. This seems to indicate that both tasks required controlled processing and a serial search of the items in the frame. The increase in memory set increases demands on capacity and performance is impaired. After extended practice the times taken in the consistent mapping condition remained nearly constant when the frame size or the memory-set size increased. This is evidence of automatic processing. The task requires so little attentional resources that the frame or memory-set size does not affect performance. In contrast, the times in the varied mapping condition continued to be affected by both variables even after extended practice. This indicates that this task still required controlled processing. Schneider and Shiffrin argue that this is because, if a controlled processing task is to become automatic, it is necessary that there is consistent mapping between the stimuli and responses. This is possible in the consistent mapping condition (where if the letter D was a target then it would never be a distracter character) but it is not possible in the varied mapping condition (where the letter D might be a target in some trials but a distracter in others).

Article 3

Hubel, D.H. (1963). The visual cortex of the brain. *Scientific American*, 210, 54–62.

Aim

This was a review article that summarised a lot of the contemporary knowledge about the neurophysiology of the visual system. Some of the content is not directly relevant here and the sections on the visual pathways, the retina and the role of the lateral geniculate body have been omitted. Only Hubel's summary of his work with Wiesel that dealt with single cells of the visual cortex is discussed. The aim of Hubel's review was to try to explain how the cells of the visual cortex are organised to detect lines and patterns in the visual field.

Method

Hubel and Wiesel used a standard procedure to record the activity of cells in the visual cortex of cats. The cats were anaesthetised and placed on a table facing a screen 1.5 metres away. Various patterns of light could be projected onto the screen. Typically the patterns were bars of light or dark (lines) at a variety of orientations. The position of these lines in the visual field could be altered (e.g. the line could be in the top left or bottom right, etc.). The cat's eyes were held open to allow the retina to be stimulated.

As the lines and patterns were shown, microelectrodes were inserted into the visual cortex. Microelectrodes are very fine and can record the activity of single cells (normal electrodes record the activity of large numbers of interconnected cells). Once a cell has been found, lines of different orientations are shown to different parts of the visual field. Two types of responses were recorded from the cells: an increase in firing activity (which indicates excitation) or a decrease in firing activity (which indicates inhibition). The process is then repeated for other cells. An important aspect of the research was to map the activity of adjoining cells.

Results

The results of the studies of the cells of the visual cortex can be summarised into two main areas: types of cell and organisation of cells.

TYPES OF CELL

Hubel describes two main types of cell in the visual cortex: simple cells and complex cells. (Hubel and Wiesel later added a third category, the hypercomplex cell.) The responses of simple cells varied from cell to cell, so that some responded best to white lines on a dark background, some responded best to dark lines on light background and others responded best to the boundary between light and dark regions. The crucial factors for all simple cells were the position and orientation of the stimulus. Simple cells only respond to stimuli in a specific region of the visual field. They also respond optimally to lines of one orientation. As the stimulus moves from this orientation the response declines rapidly.

The complex cells act in much the same way as the simple cells. They respond to different information about lines of a particular orientation. However, the crucial difference is that complex cells respond to the stimulus no matter where it is in the visual field. As long as the stimulus remains at the same orientation a complex cell responds to it.

ORGANISATION OF CELLS

The organisation of the cells was found by inserting the microelectrode at different angles into the cortex. When the electrode is inserted vertically all the cells respond to lines of the same orientation. The cells seem to be arranged in columns so that, if the first cell responds to horizontal lines, the rest of that column will also. When the electrode is inserted at an oblique angle it goes across a number of columns. This reveals a high level of organisation of the visual cortex. As the electrode passes through each column, the optimum orientation changes slightly. If cells of the first column respond best to horizontal lines, the next column responds best to lines a few degrees off horizontal, the next column a few degrees more and so on.

Discussion

These findings have great implications for any theory of pattern recognition. The fact that parts of the visual cortex are highly organised into columns of cells responding to specific information about lines of a precise orientation lends great weight to the feature detection theories. The feature detection theories suggest that patterns are recognised by analysing the individual features of the pattern. The cells described by Hubel seem to be direct neurophysiological evidence that individual lines are analysed.

However, care must be taken in interpreting the data obtained from one part of the visual system. The visual system is very complex and involves a number of stages. As Hubel puts it:

One cannot expect to 'explain' vision from the knowledge of the behaviour of a single set of cells any more than one could understand a wood-pulp mill from an examination of the machine that cuts logs into chips.

Article 4

Young, A.W., Hay, D.C. and Ellis, A.W. (1985). The faces that launched a thousand slips: everyday difficulties and errors in recognising people. *British Journal of Psychology*, 76, 495–523.

Aim

The aim of this study was to investigate the everyday errors and difficulties that people have in face recognition. Young *et al.* argued that the types of errors that are made in recognising faces could help in the understanding of the processes involved.

Twenty-two participants were asked to keep records of all the problems they encountered in face recognition over an eight-week period. This type of study is usually called a 'diary study'. The diarists were asked to record any incident, no matter how insignificant it seemed, and to record the incident as soon as possible after it had occurred. The record sheets asked for a lot of information including the following:

- Type of incident
- Source (details of the visual details available)
- General details (conditions, state of participant, how long incident lasted, etc.)
- People involved
- The way the incident ended

The first week of the eight-week period was a 'training week' to allow the participants to familiarise themselves with the recording sheets and the study.

During the seven weeks of the main study 1,008 records were obtained. Of these, 86 were 'resemblance only', where the participant thought that someone closely resembled someone else but did not make an error in recognition. The remaining 922 records were errors of recognition and were classified into seven principal types (some were further classified into sub-types). These were:

1. *Person unrecognised.* These were failures to recognise a familiar person. Sometimes these were very familiar people or people who were expected to be encountered. (114 incidents)
2. *Person misidentified.* These involved mistaking one person for another. There are two types: mistaking an unfamiliar person for a familiar one or mistaking a familiar person for another familiar person. (314 incidents)

3. *Person seemed familiar only*. There were three types of mistake in this category: a familiar person was eventually recognised; a person seemed familiar but the diarist could not remember why; and a person was found to be unfamiliar. (233 incidents)

4. *Difficulty in retrieving full details of person*. These were incidents in which the diarist could retrieve some details of a person but could not recall others. Typically this involved the inability to retrieve the name of the person. (190 incidents)

5. *Not sure if it was a particular person or not*. These involved an inability to decide whether a person had been correctly identified or not. (35 incidents)

6. *Thought it wasn't the person it was*. A familiar person was not recognised as being familiar. (4 incidents)

7. *Wrong name given to a person*. (9 incidents)

(There were a further 23 incidents which were hard to classify.)

Discussion

The results of this study seem to indicate that there are a number of stages in face recognition. Young *et al.* suggest that initially the features of faces are analysed. This analysis is then compared to some type of recognition unit. The recognition unit does not contain information about the person, only the face. Further information is stored in person identity nodes or other information stores. The study revealed that one major type of error was misidentifying a person. This presumably would happen if the wrong identity information was matched with the face recognition unit. Another major source of errors was recognising that a person was familiar but being unable to recall any details about them. This would occur if a face recognition unit was activated but the person identity node could not be accessed. The difficulties in recalling details about a person suggest that the person identity node has been accessed but that further information about the person is blocked.

Glossary

action slips. The types of errors that occur because of attention failure.

alexia. A condition that results in reading problems even though speech is understood.

apperceptive agnosia. A form of visual agnosia which impairs the ability to perceive objects.

associative agnosia. A form of visual agnosia that impairs the ability to understand the meaning or purpose of an object even though it can be perceived.

attenuation. A process that reduces the intensity of a stimulus.

automatic processing. The processing of tasks that appear to make no demands on attentional resources and therefore are fast and effortless.

bottom-up processing. Patterns are recognised by analysing the constituent parts and building up the whole picture.

cocktail party phenomenon. The observation that you can be in deep conversation with someone in a crowded room but will notice if another person mentions your name.

cognitive neuropsychology. The study of the cognitive abilities of brain-damaged patients in order to identify 'modules' of cognition (recognition of speech, face recognition, etc.).

cognitive neuroscience. The use of a variety of techniques to try to link the structure and functioning of the brain with cognitive processes.

cognitive science. The use of computer models to understand cognition.

controlled processing. The type of attentional processing used for difficult, unpractised tasks that require conscious control.

dichotic listening. A technique for studying attention in which two different messages are presented simultaneously to either ear.

divided attention. The ability to attend to two or more tasks at once.

dual task. A technique for studying attention in which participants are asked to attempt two tasks at once.

early selection. Models of attention which argue that some information is selected for analysis at an early stage of the attention process.

feature detection theories. Theories that propose that recognition of patterns occurs by the analysis of the component parts of the pattern.

focused attention. The ability to select some information from a mass of data for analysis.

geon. A 'geometric ion'. One of a limited number of simple shapes that can be combined to form all complex shapes.

late selection. Models of attention which argue that all information is processed before selection for attention and therefore selection is late in the attention process.

modular processing. The processing of information by separate sub-units of attention and perception.

parallel processing. The simultaneous processing of two or more sets of information.

pattern recognition. The ability to pick out certain parts of a stimulus to form a recognisable whole that can be matched to memory.

prosopagnosia. A disorder that impairs the ability to recognise faces.

prototypes. An idealised abstract mental pattern that is used to identify stimulus patterns.

schema. A mental representation of an action or sequence of actions.

serial processing. The processing of information in a sequential set of stages.

shadowing. A procedure used in the study of attention in which participants are asked to repeat an auditory message.

single channel models. Models of attention that assume that all attentional processes are dealt with by one processor.

Stroop effect. The interference caused when trying to name the colour of ink of words indicating a different colour (e.g. RED written in blue ink).

GLOSSARY

template theories. Theories that argue that pattern recognition involves matching a visual stimulus with a template stored in memory.

top-down processing. Patterns are recognised by forming a hypothesis about the whole pattern. This leads to recognition of the whole and subsequently the constituent parts.

References

Allport, D.A. (1980). Attention and performance. In G. Claxton (ed.) *Cognitive Psychology: New Directions.* London: Routledge & Kegan Paul.

—— (1993). Attention and control. Have we been asking the wrong questions? A critical review of twenty-five years. In D.E. Meyer and S.M. Kornblum (eds) *Attention and Performance*, vol. XIV. London: MIT Press.

Allport, D.A., Antonis, B. and Reynolds, P. (1972). On the division of attention: a disproof of the single channel hypothesis. *Quarterly Journal of Experimental Psychology*, 24, 225–35.

Baddeley, A.D. (1986). *Working Memory.* Oxford: Oxford University Press.

—— (1993). Working memory or working attention? In A.D. Baddeley and L. Wieskrantz (eds) *Attention: Selection, Awareness, and Control. A Tribute to Donald Broadbent.* Oxford: Clarendon Press.

Biederman, I. (1987). Recognition by components: a theory of human image understanding. *Psychological Review*, 94, 115–47.

Broadbent, D.E. (1954). The role of auditory localisation and attention in memory span. *Journal of Experimental Psychology*, 47, 191–6.

—— (1958). *Perception and Communication.* Oxford: Pergamon.

Brown, E., Deffenbacher, K. and Sturgill, W. (1977). Memory for faces and the circumstances of encounter. *Journal of Applied Psychology*, 62, 311–18.

Bruce, V. (1988). *Recognising Faces.* Hove, UK: Lawrence Erlbaum Associates Ltd.

Bruce, V. and Burton, M. (1989). Computer recognition of faces. In H.D. Ellis and A.W. Young (eds) *Handbook of Research on Face Processing.* North-Holland: Elsevier Science.

Bruce, V. and Young, A. (1986). Understanding face recognition. *British Journal of Psychology*, 77, 305–27.

—— (1998). *In the Eye of the Beholder: The Science of Face Perception.* Oxford: Oxford University Press.

Bruce, V., Green, P.R. and Georgeson, M.A. (1996). *Visual Perception: Physiology, Psychology, and Ecology* (3rd edn). Hove, UK: Psychology Press.

Bruyer, R., Laterre, C., Seron, X., Feyereisen, P., Strypstein, E., Pierrard, E. and Rectem, D. (1983). A case of prosopagnosia with some preserved covert remembrance of familiar faces. *Brain and Cognition*, 2, 257–84.

Burton, A.M. and Bruce, V. (1992). I recognise your face but I can't remember your name. A simple explanation? *British Journal of Psychology*, 83, 45–60.

Burton, A.M., Bruce, V. and Johnson, R.A. (1990). Understanding face recognition with an interactive activation model. *British Journal of Psychology*, 81, 361–80.

Cheng, P.W. (1985). Restructuring versus automaticity: alternative accounts of skills acquisition. *Psychological Review*, 92, 414–23.

Cherry, E.C. (1953). Some experiments on the recognition of speech with one and two ears. *Journal of the Acoustic Society of America*, 25, 975–9.

Davies, G.M., Ellis, H.D. and Shepperd, J.W. (1978). Face identification: the influence of delay upon accuracy of a photofit construction. *Journal of Police Science and Administration*, 6, 35–42.

Dawson, M.E. and Schell, A.M. (1982). Electrodermal responses to attended and nonattended significant stimuli during dichotic listening. *Journal of Experimental Psychology: Human Perception and Performance*, 8, 315–24.

de Hann, E.H.F., Young, A.W. and Newcombe, F. (1991). A dissociation between the sense of familiarity and access to semantic information concerning familiar people. *European Journal of Cognitive Psychology*, 3, 51–67.

DeRenzi, E. (1986). Current issues on prosopagnosia. In H.D. Ellis, M.A. Jeeves, F. Newcombe and A. Young (eds) *Aspects of Face Processing*. Dordrecht: Nijhoff.

Desimone, R. (1991). Face-selective cells in the temporal cortex of monkeys. *Journal of Cognitive Neuroscience*, 3, 1–8.

Deutsch, J.A. and Deutsch, D. (1963). Attention: some theoretical considerations. *Psychological Review*, 70, 80–90.

—— (1967). Comments on 'Selective attention: perceptions or response?' *Quarterly Journal of Experimental Psychology*, 19, 362–3.

Devlin, Lord Patrick (1976). *Report to the Secretary of State for the Home Department of the Departmental Committee on Evidence of Identification in Criminal Cases*. London: HMSO.

Ellis, A.W. and Young, A.W. (1989). *Human Cognitive Neuropsychology*. Hove, UK: Lawrence Erlbaum Associates Ltd.

Ellis, A.W., Burton, A.M., Young, A. and Flude, B.M. (1997). Repetition priming between parts and wholes: tests of a computational model of familiar face recognition. *British Journal of Psychology*, 88, 579–608.

Ellis, H.D. and Young, A.W. (1989). Are faces special? In H.D. Ellis and A.W. Young (eds) *Handbook of Research on Face Processing*. North-Holland: Elsevier Science.

Ellis, H.D., Davies, G.M. and Shepherd, J.W. (1978). A critical examination of the Photofit system for recalling faces. *Ergonomics*, 21, 297–307.

Ellis, H.D., Shepherd, J.W. and Davies, G.M. (1979). Identification of familiar and unfamiliar faces from internal and external features: some implications for theories of face recognition. *Perception*, 8, 431–9.

Eysenck, M.W. (1984). *A Handbook of Cognitive Psychology*. Hove, UK: Lawrence Erlbaum Associates Ltd.

Eysenck, M.W. (1993). *Principles of Cognitive Psychology*. Hove, UK: Lawrence Erlbaum Associates Ltd.

Eysenck, M.W. and Keane, M.T. (1995). *Cognitive Psychology – A Student's Handbook* (3rd edn). Hove, UK: Lawrence Erlbaum Associates Ltd.

Eysenck, M.W. and Keane, M.T. (2000). *Cognitive Psychology – A Student's Handbook* (4th edn). Hove, UK: Psychology Press.

Farah, M.J. (1990). *Visual Agnosia: Disorders of Object Recognition and What They Tell Us About Normal Vision.* Cambridge, MA: MIT Press.

Farah, M.J. (1994). Specialisation within visual object recognition: clues from prosopagnosia and alexia. In M.J. Farah and G. Ratcliff (eds) *The Neuropsychology of High-level Vision: Collected Tutorial Essays.* Hillsdale, NJ: Lawrence Erlbaum Associates Inc.

Farah, M.J., Wilson, K.D., Drain, M. and Tanaka, J.N. (1998). What is 'special' about face perception? *Psychological Review,* 105, 482–98.

Farah, M.J. (2000). Interview with Martha Farah. *Journal of Cognitive Neuroscience,* 12, 360–3.

Fisk, A.D. and Hodge, K.A. (1992). Retention of trained performance in consistent mapping search after extended delay. *Human Factors,* 34, 147–64.

Flude, B.M., Ellis, A.W. and Kay, J. (1989). Face processing and name retrieval in an anomic aphasia: names are stored separately from semantic information about people. *Brain and Cognition,* 11, 60–72.

Gray, J.A. and Wedderburn, A.A. (1960). Grouping strategies with simultaneous stimuli. *Quarterly Journal of Experimental Psychology,* 12, 180–4.

Greene, J. and Hicks, C. (1984). *Basic Cognitive Processes.* Milton Keynes: Open University Press.

Haig, N.D. (1984). The effect of feature displacement on face recognition. *Perception,* 13, 505–12.

Hampson, P.J. and Morris, P.E. (1996). *Understanding Cognition.* Oxford: Blackwell.

Hay, D.C. and Young, A.W. (1982). The human face. In A.W. Ellis (ed.) *Normality and Pathology in Cognitive Functions.* London: Academic Press.

Healy, A.F. (1976). Detection errors on the word *the*: evidence for reading units larger than letters. *Journal of Experimental Psychology: Human Perception and Performance,* 2, 235–42.

Henderson, J. (1999). *Memory and Forgetting.* London: Routledge.

Homa, D., Haver, B. and Schwartz, T. (1976). Perceptibility of schematic face stimuli: evidence for a perceptual Gestalt. *Memory and Cognition,* 4, 176–85.

Hubel, D.H. (1963). The visual cortex of the brain. *Scientific American,* 210, 54–62.

Hubel, D.H. and Wiesel, T.N. (1959). Receptive fields of single neurons in the cat's striate cortex. *Journal of Physiology*, 148, 574–91.

—— (1965). Receptive fields of single neurons in the two non-striate visual areas, 18 and 19 of the cat. *Journal of Neurophysiology*, 28, 229–89.

—— (1968). Receptive fields and functional architecture of monkey striate cortex. *Journal of Physiology*, 195, 215–43.

Inhoff, A.W. and Topolski, R. (1994). Seeing morphemes: loss of visibility during the retinal stabilisation of compound and pseudocompound words. *Journal of Experimental Psychology: Human Perception and Performance*, 20, 840–53.

Ishai, A., Ungerleider, L.G., Martin, A., Schouten, J.L. and Haxby, J.V. (1999). Distributed representation of objects in the human ventral visual pathway. *Proceedings of the National Academy of Science*, 96, 9379–9384.

James, W. (1890). *The Principles of Psychology*. New York: Henry Holt & Company.

Johnson, W.A. and Heinz, S.P. (1978). Flexibility and capacity demands of attention. *Journal of Experimental Psychology: General*, 107, 420–35.

—— (1979). Depth of non-target processing in an attention task. *Journal of Experimental Psychology*, 5, 168–75.

Kahneman, D. (1973). *Attention and Effort*. Englewood Cliffs, NJ: Prentice Hall.

Leeper, R.W. (1935). A study of a neglected portion of the field of learning: the development of sensory organisation. *Journal of Genetic Psychology*, 46, 41–75.

Logan, G.D. (1988). Toward an instance theory of automatisation. *Psychological Review*, 95, 492–527.

MacKay, D.G. (1973). Aspects of the theory of comprehension, memory and attention. *Quarterly Journal of Experimental Psychology*, 25, 22–40.

Malone, D.R., Morris, H.H., Kay, M.C. and Levin, H.S. (1982). Prosopagnosia: a double dissociation between the recognition of familiar and unfamiliar faces. *Journal of Neurology, Neurosurgery and Psychiatry*, 45, 820–2.

Manly, T., Robertson, I.H., Galloway, M. and Hawkins, K. (1999). The absent mind: further investigations of sustained attention to response. *Neuropsychologia*, 37, 661–70.

Mollon, J.D. (1982). Colour vision. *Annual Review of Psychology*, 33, 41–85.

Moray, N. (1959). Attention in dichotic listening: affective cues and the influence of instructions. *Quarterly Journal of Experimental Psychology*, 11, 56–60.

Navon, D. and Gopher, D. (1979). On the economy of the human processing system. *Psychological Review*, 86, 214–55.

Neisser, U. (1964). Visual search. *Scientific American*, 210, 94–102.

Neisser, U. (1976). *Cognition and Reality: Principles and Implications of Cognitive Psychology*. San Francisco: Freeman.

Neuman, O. (1984). Automatic processing: a review of recent findings and a plea for an old theory. In W. Printz and A. Sanders (eds) *Cognition and Motor Processes*. Berlin: Springer.

Norman, D.A. (1969). Memory while shadowing. *Quarterly Journal of Experimental Psychology*, 21, 85–93.

—— (1976). *Memory and Attention* (2nd edn). Chichester: Wiley.

Norman, D.A. and Bobrow, D.G. (1975). On data-limited and resource-limited processes. *Cognitive Psychology*, 7, 44–64.

Norman, D.A. and Shallice, T. (1986). Attention to action: willed and automatic control of behaviour. In R.J. Davidson, G.E. Schwartz and D. Shapiro (eds) *The Design of Everyday Things*. New York: Doubleday.

Payne, D.G. and Wenger, M.J. (1998). *Cognitive Psychology*. Boston: Houghton Mifflin.

Perrett, D.I., Mistlin, A.J., Potter, D.D., Smith, P.A.J., Head, A.S., Chitty, A.J., Broennimann, R., Milner, A.D. and Jeeves, M.A.J. (1986). Functional organisation of visual neurones processing face identity. In H.D. Ellis, M.A. Jeeves, F. Newcombe and A. Young (eds) *Aspects of Face Processing*. Dordrecht: Nijhoff.

Perrett, D.I., Harries, M.H., Mistlin, A.J., Hietanen, J.K., Benson, P.J., Bevan, R., Thomas, S., Oram, M.W., Ortega, J. and Brierly, K. (1990). Social signals analysed at the single cell level: someone is looking at me, something touched me, something moved. *International Journal of Comparative Psychology*, 4, 25–55.

Posner, M.I. and Snyder, C.R.R. (1975). Attention and cognitive control. In R.L. Solso (ed.) *Information Processing and Cognition: The Loyola Symposium*. Hillsdale, NJ: Lawrence Erlbaum Associates Inc.

Reason, J.T. (1979). Actions not as planned: the price of automatisation.

In G. Underwood and R. Stevens (eds) *Aspects of Consciousness: Vol. 1. Psychological Issues.* London: Academic Press.

—— (1990). *Human Error.* Cambridge, Mass: Cambridge University Press.

—— (1992). Cognitive underspecification: its variety and consequences. In B.J. Baars (ed.) *Experimental Slips and Error: Exploring the Architecture of Volition.* New York: Plenum Press.

Robertson, I.H., Manly, T., Andrade, J., Baddeley, B .T. and Yiend, J. (1997a). 'Oops!': Performance correlates of everyday attentional failures in traumatic brain injured and normal subjects. *Neuropsychologia*, 35, 6, 747–58.

Robertson, I.H., Ridgeway, V., Greenfield, E. and Parr, A. (1997b). Motor recovery after stroke depends on intact sustained attention: a two-year follow-up study. *Neuropsychology*, 11, 290–5.

Rookes, P. and Wilson, J. (2000). *Perception.* London: Routledge.

Schneider, W. and Shiffrin, R.M. (1977). Controlled and automatic human information processing: detection, search and attention. *Psychological Review*, 84, 1–66.

Selfridge, O.G. (1959). Pandemonium: a paradigm for learning. In D.V. Blake and A.M. Utley (eds) *Symposium on the Mechanisms of Thought Processes.* London: HMSO.

Sellen, A.J. and Norman, D.A. (1992). The psychology of slips. In B.J. Baars (ed.) *Experimental Slips and Human Error: Exploring the Architecture of Volition.* New York: Plenum Press.

Shepherd, J.W., Davies, G.M. and Ellis, H.D. (1981). Studies of cue saliency. In G. Davies, H. Ellis and J. Shepherd (eds) *Perceiving and Remembering Faces.* Dordrecht: Nijhoff.

Shiffrin, R.M. and Schneider, W. (1977). Controlled and automatic human information processing: II. Perceptual learning, automatic attending, and a general theory. *Psychological Review*, 84, 127–90.

Solso, R.L. (1979). *Cognitive Psychology.* New York: Harcourt Brace Jovanovich.

—— (1998). *Cognitive Psychology* (5th edn). Boston: Allyn & Bacon.

Spelke, E.S., Hirst, W.C. and Neisser, U. (1976). Skills of divided attention. *Cognition*, 4, 215–30.

Stroop, J.R. (1935). Studies of interference in serial-verbal reaction. *Journal of Experimental Psychology*, 18, 643–62.

Styles, E.A. (1997). *The Psychology of Attention.* Hove, UK: Psychology Press.

Treisman, A.M. (1964). Verbal cues, language and meaning in selective attention. *American Journal of Psychology*, 77, 206–19.

Treisman, A.M. and Davies, A. (1973). Divided attention to ear and eye. In S. Kornblum (ed.) *Attention and Performance IV.* London: Academic Press.

Treisman, A.M. and Geffen, G. (1967). Selective attention: perception or response. *Quarterly Journal of Experimental Psychology*, 19, 1–18.

Treisman, A.M. and Schmidt, H. (1982). Illusory conjunctions in the perception of objects. *Cognitive Psychology*, 14, 107–41.

Turk, M. and Pentland, A. (1991). Eigenfaces for recognition. *Journal of Cognitive Neuroscience,* 3, 71–86.

Underwood, G. (1974). Moray vs. the rest: the effects of extended shadowing practice. *Quarterly Journal of Experimental Psychology*, 26, 368–72.

Wheeler, D.D. (1970). Processes in word recognition. *Cognitive Psychology*, 1, 59–85.

Wickens, C.D. (1984). Processing resources in attention. In R. Parasuraman and D.R. Davies (eds) *Varieties of Attention.* London: Academic Press.

Wickens, C.D., Sandry, D. and Vidulich, M. (1983). Compatibility and resource competition between modalities of input, output, and central processing. *Human Factors*, 26, 227–48.

Young, A. and Bruce, V. (1991). Perceptual categories and the computation of 'Grandmother'. *European Journal of Cognitive Psychology*, 3, 5–49.

—— (1998). *Face and Mind.* Oxford: Oxford University Press.

Young, A.W., Hay, D.C. and Ellis, A.W. (1985). The faces that launched a thousand slips: everyday difficulties and errors in recognising people. *British Journal of Psychology*, 76, 495–523.

Young, A.W., Hellawell, D. and Hay, D.C. (1987). Configural information in face processing. *Perception*, 16, 747–59.

Index